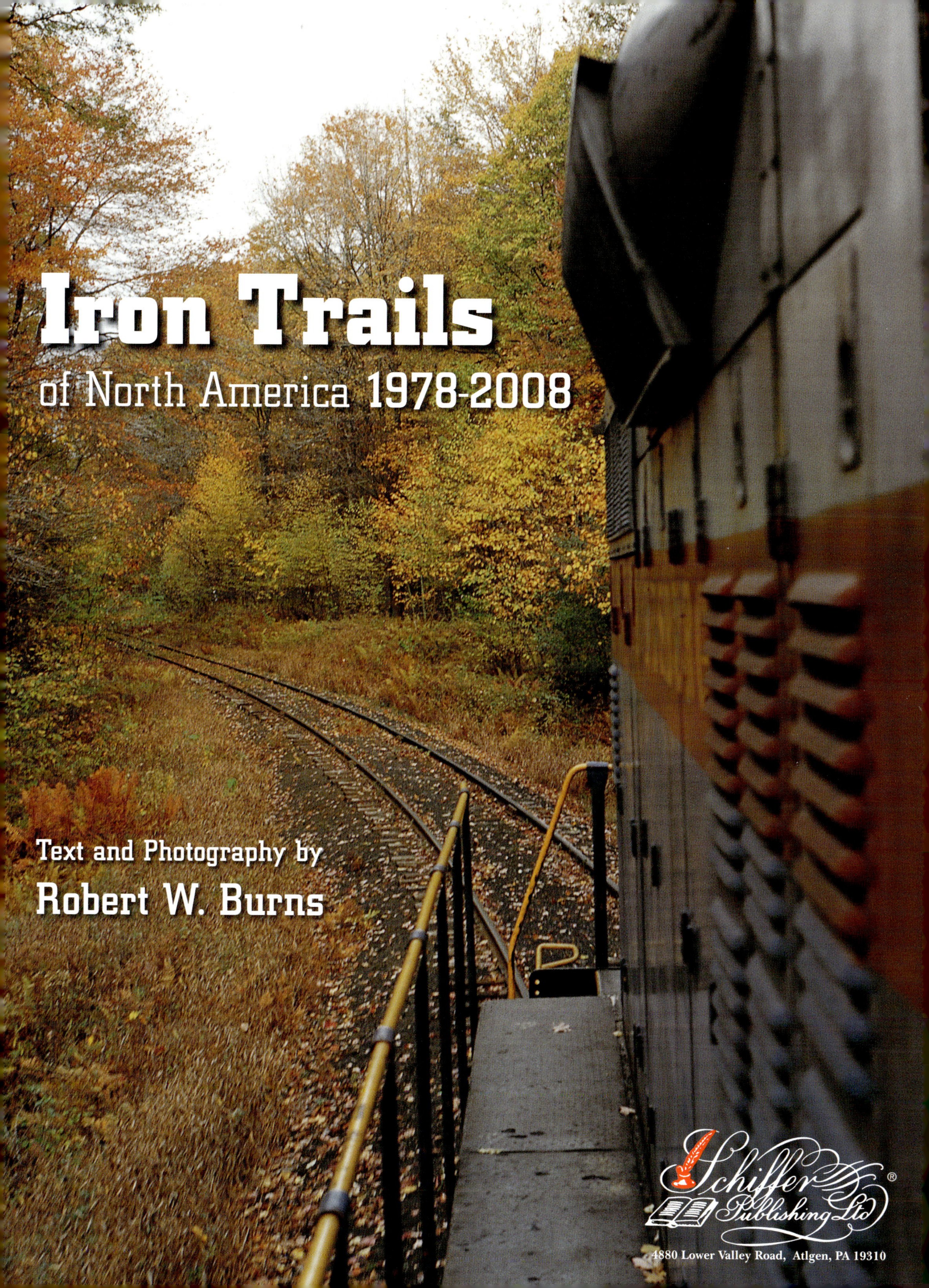
Iron Trails
of North America 1978-2008
Text and Photography by
Robert W. Burns
Schiffer Publishing Ltd
4880 Lower Valley Road, Atlgen, PA 19310

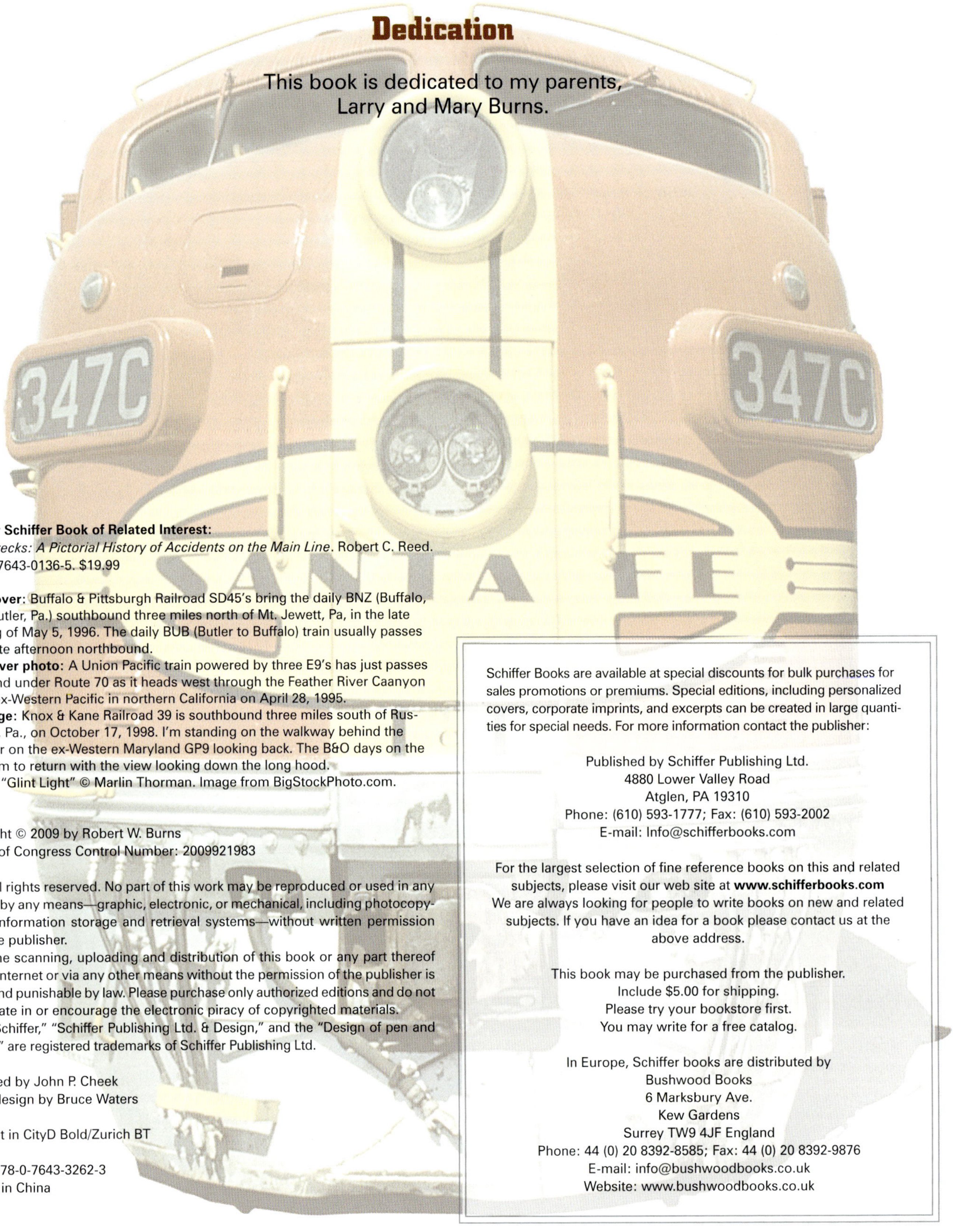

Dedication

This book is dedicated to my parents,
Larry and Mary Burns.

Another Schiffer Book of Related Interest:
Train Wrecks: A Pictorial History of Accidents on the Main Line. Robert C. Reed.
ISBN:0-7643-0136-5. $19.99

Front cover: Buffalo & Pittsburgh Railroad SD45's bring the daily BNZ (Buffalo, NY to Butler, Pa.) southbound three miles north of Mt. Jewett, Pa, in the late morning of May 5, 1996. The daily BUB (Butler to Buffalo) train usually passes in the late afternoon northbound.
Back cover photo: A Union Pacific train powered by three E9's has just passes Pulga and under Route 70 as it heads west through the Feather River Caanyon on the ex-Western Pacific in northern California on April 28, 1995.
Title page: Knox & Kane Railroad 39 is southbound three miles south of Russell City, Pa., on October 17, 1998. I'm standing on the walkway behind the engineer on the ex-Western Maryland GP9 looking back. The B&O days on the line seem to return with the view looking down the long hood.
Page 6: "Glint Light" © Marlin Thorman. Image from BigStockPhoto.com.

Library of Congress Control Number: 2009921983

Designed by John P. Cheek
Cover design by Bruce Waters

Type set in CityD Bold/Zurich BT

ISBN: 978-0-7643-3262-3
Printed in China

Schiffer Books are available at special discounts for bulk purchases for sales promotions or premiums. Special editions, including personalized covers, corporate imprints, and excerpts can be created in large quantities for special needs. For more information contact the publisher:

Published by Schiffer Publishing Ltd.
4880 Lower Valley Road
Atglen, PA 19310
Phone: (610) 593-1777; Fax: (610) 593-2002
E-mail: Info@schifferbooks.com

For the largest selection of fine reference books on this and related subjects, please visit our web site at **www.schifferbooks.com**
We are always looking for people to write books on new and related subjects. If you have an idea for a book please contact us at the above address.

This book may be purchased from the publisher.
Include $5.00 for shipping.
Please try your bookstore first.
You may write for a free catalog.

In Europe, Schiffer books are distributed by
Bushwood Books
6 Marksbury Ave.
Kew Gardens
Surrey TW9 4JF England
Phone: 44 (0) 20 8392-8585; Fax: 44 (0) 20 8392-9876
E-mail: info@bushwoodbooks.co.uk
Website: www.bushwoodbooks.co.uk

Preface

Many times I have been asked, "Why the interest in railroads?", and I don't think I ever once fully answered the question. One example happened when I was going to fly to Las Vegas on vacation. A person from work asked me what the plan was for when I arrived. First thing was to get a rental car at the airport and head south on Route 95 for 90 miles to the Santa Fe's Los Angeles-to-Chicago mainline west of Needles, California, and spend the next week following and photographing the line to Winslow, Arizona. I remember a complete blank look on his face.

There was not one thing, but a combination of many circumstances over the years, that helped the interest develop. From my first Marx 0-scale New Haven train set at Christmas, 1963, to my granddad Archie Burns and great uncle John Burns, who told stories of their railroad days, trains on the B & O branchline to Mt. Jewett, Pennsylvania, train excursions and Amtrak trips; the list could go on and on.

This book wasn't planned, but is the result of thirty years of rail photography. Not always easy to achieve, some of the photos would be made by chance as I just happened to arrive at a location with moments to set up for a shot. Other photos would require hours and sometimes days going back to the location to get the intended shot. On light density lines, such as the Buffalo & Pittsburgh line through Mt. Jewett, an hour or two delay could drastically change lighting conditions, and that one little cloud in the sky has more than once covered up the sun just as the train came into view. If the photo didn't work out that day, it took another 80-mile round trip the following day to achieve better results.

Change has always been a part of railroading, and the last thirty years have been no exception. Looking over these photos, even though in many cases the lines are still in operation, it is surprising to see mow many of the old and newer railroads have been lost to mergers.

The railroad industry, for the most part, is hidden from the majority of the people. Other than the inconvenience of waiting at a grade crossing or news of a derailment, most people don't give trains a second look. But the more you travel around the railroads, the more that "I didn't know that" things begin to add up and slowly they make you realize that American railroads are an interesting diversion.

Looking back, I cannot think of not knowing or not having been to the locations shown on these pages. Hopefully, the next time someone asks about why the interest, the book will be able to explain to their satisfaction.

My granddad Archie and great uncle John would both start out on the Tionesta Valley Railway (my granddad later went to the Pennsylvania Railroad, my uncle to the Buffalo, Rochester and Pittsburgh Railway). I had to show two photos of their railroad. Nearly fifty years after the railroad's demise, one of their wooden cabooses rested near Cherry Run four miles south of Sheffield, Pennsylvania, on October 29, 1989. Minus its trucks, its second life as a camp has long-since been over. Over the years, I've managed to find enough pieces along the abandoned grade to assemble a sixteen-foot section of the three-foot gauge line seen at Brookston, Pennsylvania, on July 15, 2005.

Acknowledgment

I offer special thanks to Bonnie Curry and Bonnie Anderson for taking my hand-written material and putting it in order for this book.

The E8 was EMD's most successful passenger locomotive. Between 1949 and 1953, 454 A units and 35 B units were built. Powered by two V-12 567's, the locomotive developed 2,250 horsepower. The Pennsylvania Railroad took delivery of 74 A units between 1950 and 1952. The success of the earlier E7's over the other manufactures' passenger locomotive convinced Pennsy to return to GM. The two pictured here are: 5711 built in October 1952, and 5809 built in January 1951. These two engines worked for Pennsy on their long distance passenger trains until the ill-fated merger with New York Central in 1968, forming Penn Central. With the creation of Amtrak in 1971, the freight railroads were finally able to rid themselves of the money-loosing passenger trains they were forced to continue to operate. The two Pennsy E8's were transferred to Amtrak. In 1983, Conrail obtained the two former Pennsy E8's to go along with another E8, former Erie Railroad 833. The three engines powered Conrail inspection trains. With the breakup of Conrail in 1999, one went to Norfolk Southern and two to CSX. The two railroads had no interest in the engines. In June 2000, former 5809 were auctioned off at Altoona to Bennett Levin. He later purchased ex-5711 and ex-833. Both Pennsy engines were restored to their late 1950s appearance, with Tuscan red paint, a single gold stripe, and large Pennsylvania road name. The four portholes along each side of the car body were restored and the distinctive Pennsy train phone antennas that run the full length of the roof were reconstructed. Above, 5809 and 5711 are at Altoona Pa. on October 6, 2001. They ran from Philadelphia earlier in the day and ran excursion trains around the Horseshoe Curve to Gallitzin on October 6th and 7th for Altoona Railfest Weekend 2001. The E8's head a private passenger car train west at Youngsville, Pa. on August 19, 2001on the former Pennsy Erie to Emporium line, now Buffalo & Pittsburgh. The train ran from Philadelphia west to Harrisburg, up Norfolk Southern's ex-Pennsy Buffalo Mainline to Emporium, west to Erie on the Allegheny and Eastern, west to Conneaut, Ohio on CSX, south to Butler on the Bessemer and Lake Erie, south to Pittsburgh on the North Bessemer and Union Railroads, returning north to Butler, then running east to Falls Creek on the Buffalo and Pittsburgh Railroad, east on the old Pennsy low grade line to Driftwood, where the train rejoined the Buffalo Mainline to Harrisburg and Philadelphia. This was a three-day trip. It had been over 36 years since the last Pennsy E8 powered a passenger train operated, on the Erie to Emporium line on March 27, 1965. Earlier in the 20th century, the Pennsylvania Railroad was the transportation leader in the United States, moving ten percent of the rail traffic with only four percent of the U.S. route mileage. Little wonder today that when these engines operate they have the ability to draw thousands trackside, from older people who have known the railroad to kids who were born years after Pennsy's demise. For a few moments they get a glimpse at what once was the "Standard Railroad of the World."

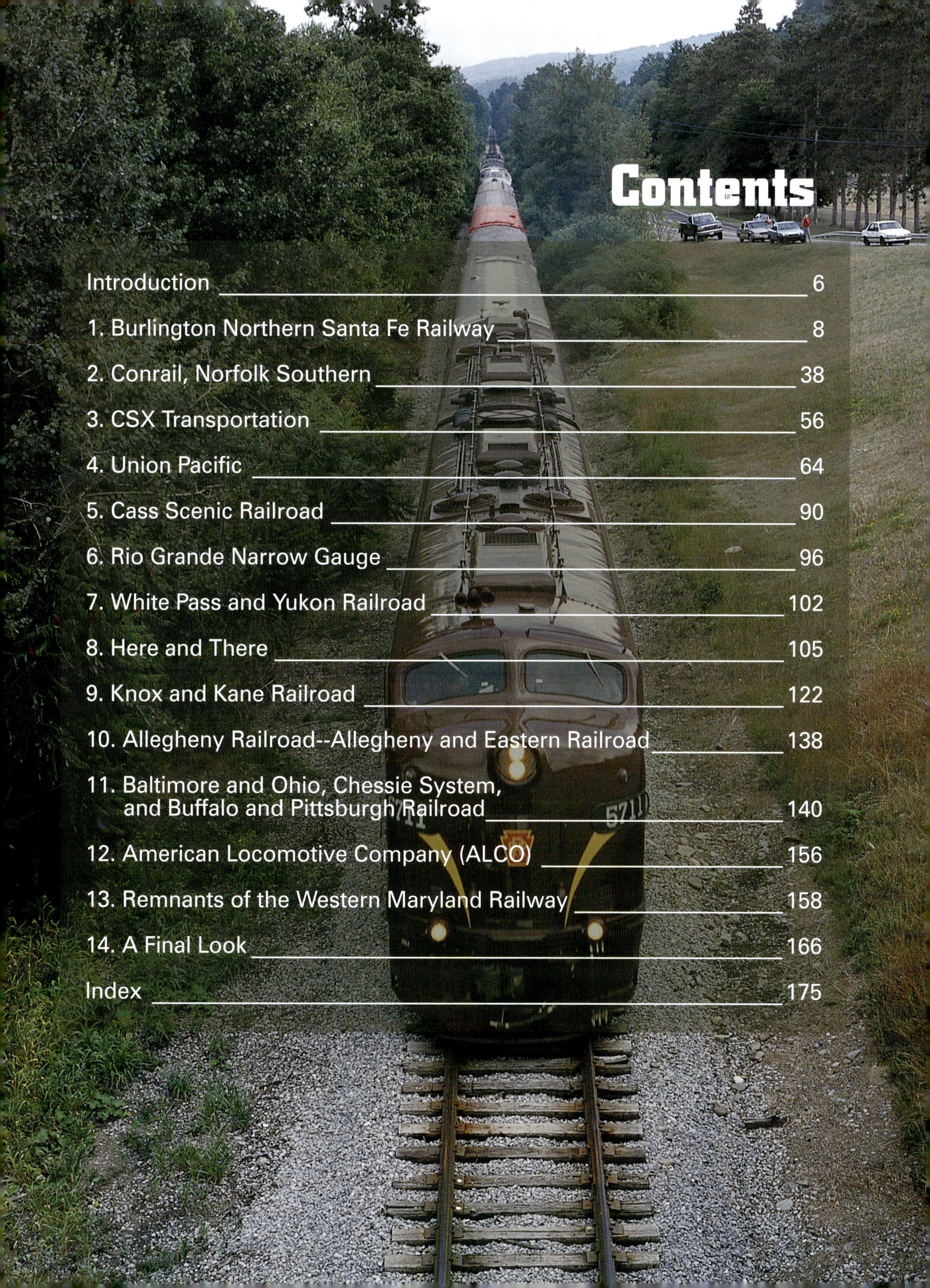

Contents

Introduction

This book presents North American railroads from 1978 to 2008. Many changes took place when the Staggers Rail Act was passed in 1980. Since 1889, the Interstate Commerce Commission had to approve any rate changes the railroads wanted to change, either higher or lower. Since 1980, railroads could set their own rates. Also, the act made procedures easier for railroads to merge and abandon lines. Many of the cast-off lines became regional and short-line railroads. Traffic levels began to pick up, and as they did the railroads were faced with a new problem; many of their lines were running at full capacity.

Since the 1950s, mainly the Midwest and Northeast railroads had slowly been abandoning and downgrading lines due to traffic lost by increased use of the Interstate Highway System and industries relocating to the South and West. But now, millions would have to be spent on locomotives, cars, and track to increase capacity and millions more for future growth. By the end of the 1990s, four railroads controlled most of the U.S. traffic: Burlington Northern Santa Fe, Union Pacific, Norfolk Southern, and CSX.

Railroads' resurgence may be due to their ability to haul freight at 1/3 the fuel cost of travel by highway. As one looks at a steel wheel setting on a steel rail, there is just a slight point of contact with the two, causing the least resistance of any form of land transportation. As the cost of oil exploration increases, and with continued trouble in the Mid-East, railroads will prove more important in future transportation needs.

But as to competition on a time basis, the rails never will beat a truck's delivery time. As an example, a truck running from the east coast to Chicago may only have one pickup and one drop-off point. As soon as the trailer is sealed, and the truck hits the interstate ramp, it has a 65 mph run to Chicago. A mixed train of 100 cars may have 100 different starting and a 100 different destination points. The train must be assembled with cars coming from numerous switching crews from local industries. Once assembled and inspected, the train departs. A train may encounter five or six cities with restricted speed limits and may have car set-outs or pick-ups to make, and other switching moves at smaller towns en route. If the line is single track, numerous meets with other trains will consume more time.

Railroading's ability to haul bulk shipments is unmatched by any other land transportation. A case in point is a coal train heading from Wyoming's Powder River coal region to Chicago. A 130-car train, in which each car hauls five truck loads, takes the load of 650 trucks. A train may have five crew changes in its travel east, with ten people handling the train, instead of 650 truck drivers. The price of fuel and extra people involved in transporting the coal by truck would make the cost of Powder River coal out of reach for eastern power plants. The same goes for bulk shipments of grain shipped from the mid-west to the Atlantic, Gulf, and Pacific coasts.

Knox & Kane Railroad 2-8-2 58 is returning southbound from a Kinzua Bridge excursion at the small rock cut one-half mile north of Watson Farm, Pa., on October 20, 1990.

Chapter 1
Burlington Northern Santa Fe Railway

With the merger of the Burlington Northern and Santa Fe railways on Dec. 31, 1996, the 33,500-mile BNSF Railway was created.

The Santa Fe had its beginnings in 1860 when the Atchison and Topeka Railroad was chartered, and rails between these two Kansas cities were laid. The railroad was renamed Atchison, Topeka and Santa Fe in 1863, and rails slowly headed west to Albuquerque, New Mexico. Strangely enough, the mainline never reached Santa Fe. A branch line was built from Lamy 18 miles to reach the city. By the time of the merger with Burlington Northern in 1996, the Santa Fe line still did not reach its namesake city, having sold the branch line to a short-line operator that renamed the line Santa Fe Southern Railway.

From Albuquerque, rails were laid to Needles, California, by 1883. The Southern Pacific line to Barstow was used to connect with the California Southern Railroad that ran to San Diego. The line between Needles and Barstow was eventually purchased from Southern Pacific. Los Angeles was reached in 1887 and San Francisco in 1900.

Chicago was reached in 1888, and soon the Gulf of Mexico, with a line south from Kansas through Fort Worth to Galveston. The Belen Cutoff east of Albuquerque through central New Mexico, northern Texas, and Oklahoma to Wichita and Kansas City became Santa Fe's main freight route to southern California. The northern route, up 3.5% Raton Pass, handled most of the Santa Fe west coast passenger trains. By the 1930s Santa Fe operated 13,500 miles of track.

Burlington Northern was created on March 1, 1970, with the merger of the Great Northern (8,274 Miles), Northern Pacific (6,771 miles), Chicago, Burlington and Quincy (10,289 miles), and the Spokane, Portland & Seattle Railway (992 miles). On November 21, 1980, the Frisco (4,540 miles) was absorbed into the system to create a 22,300-mile railroad, by the time of the merger with the Santa Fe.

With the mega mergers in the 1990s, many felt that railroads had become too large to operate efficiently. To operate and maintain a system like BNSF, which covers two-thirds of the continental United States, must be a monumental task. Besides, Union Pacific, which covers much of the same territory, is always waiting the chance to take away traffic from BNSF with lower shipping rates. But competition has always been a part of railroading; shippers benefit from the lower shipping cost and railroads with increased tonnage.

A remnant of a triple meet on the Santa Fe mainline, west of Kansas City, as it happened on May 27, 1983. I was standing in the last car of the Southwest Chief. To the left is GP38 3548 with an eastbound freight, while to the right another freight heads west.

Santa Fe F7 347C rests at the California State Railroad Museum at Sacramento, California, on September 15, 1993.

Arguably the most famous face in 20th century railroading has to be the Santa Fe Warbonnet, designed in 1937 for Santa Fe's new passenger train diesels. From the E1's of the late 1930s through the late 1960s, with the purchase of General Electric's U28CG, U30CG, and EMD FP45's, the Warbonnet would endure. After Amtrak took over of national passenger service in 1971, the newer General Electric (GE) and General Motors (GM) locomotives were repainted into Santa Fe's blue and yellow for freight service. Surprisingly, in 1989, management decided to repaint 16 FP45's back to the old scheme, and would continue on every new engine from GE and GM through 1997. In May 1990, GP60M's started arriving on the Santa Fe painted in Warbonnet. The 3800 horsepower (hp.) GMs would eventually number 63, with 23 cabless GP60B's ordered in 1991.
Ten miles east of Flagstaff, Az. BNSF GP60M 128 heads west with a double stack train on Oct. 4, 1997. In a three-hour period, this was one of eight westbound and five eastbound trains that passed. Since the merger, traffic has increased on this line to around 100 trains a day.

These four photos were taken on the same day and location as the previous photo of GP60M 128. A westbound train is lead by GE DASH9-44CW 661. Santa Fe ordered 130 of these six-axle, 4400 hp. units in 1994. From the east at Winslow, Az. (4843′ elevation), the line climbs west for 96 miles with a ruling grade of 1.5% until the Arizona Divide is reached at 7334′.

SD40-2 5116 and BN SD40-2's have another westbound train. The engineer has cardboard as a makeshift sun visor to block the setting sun. The old Santa Fe mainline is the shortest route from Chicago to southern California, at 2222 miles. Three-fourths of the traffic on this line is containers and trailers, making this line BNSF's busiest intermodal route.

Two ex-BN SD40-2's with a BNSF SD75M roll a westbound double stack train. The ex-BN SD40-2's and C30-7's weren't liked by the Santa Fe crews, because of their lack of air conditioning and many of the older engines having millions of miles on them. With the Santa Fe's high speeds and rough and hot terrain, if a locomotive is ready for a breakdown, it will happen here.

DASH 9-44CW 675 heads east with boxcars, DASH8-40CW 801 follows, and two more BN SD40-2's. Santa Fe was the only railroad that had a direct line from Chicago to California, and for years the company advertised this fact on the sides of its boxcars with the slogan, "Ship and Travel Santa Fe all the Way."

GP60M 162 and GM Electro-Motive Division Leasing SD40's 6507 and 6417 haul an empty coil steel train eastbound five miles east of Seligman, Az, on October 4, 1997. It is about to pass under old Route 66.

A westbound train lead by SD45 5335 drops downhill from the Arizona Divide with the San Francisco Mountains in the background at the same location, but in Santa Fe days on April 26, 1995.

DASH8-40BW 563 is on a westbound train coming into Seligman on April 24, 1995. Santa Fe in 1990 started buying four-axle engines like the GM GP60M's and GE 4000 hp DASH8-40 BW's, but switched to six-axle units in 1992 and stayed with the six-axle units through the BNSF merger. This line, between Winslow, Az. and Needles, Ca. is known as the Seligman Subdivision.

DASH8-40CW 876 leads one of the four westbounds that was being held up east of Seligman on April 24, 1995. Track crews had the westbound main out of service, as 876 and three older six-axle GM's roll by on the eastbound main. By the time of the merger with Burlington Northern, Santa Fe's mileage was 9,126 miles, down from a one-time high of 13,500 miles.

Plans to photograph a GP60M on an eastbound are changed as three six-axle GM's head west with a double stack, 20 miles west of Seligman on October 4, 1997. Although Santa Fe's famed passenger trains have long since departed, Amtrak still operates the daily east- and westbound Chicago to Los Angeles Southwest Chief.

GP60M 101, GP40X 3805, and BN SD40-2 7160 are on an eastbound, five miles east of Seligman on October 4, 1997. 3805 is one of only 10 GP40X's Santa Fe received in 1978.The four-axle engine had GM's new 16-645F3 3,500 hp engine, and were basically test models for GM's GP50s, which started production in the early 1980s.

Three six-axle GE's have an eastbound stack train 20 mules west of Seligman, on April 26, 1995. Santa Fe introduced in 1968 its Super C premium service piggyback trains. These high-speed trains ran the LA to Chicago route on a 40 hour schedule with speeds to 90 mph. By the end of the 1970s, the service was suspended; shippers wanted the lower rates and were willing to settle for slower transit time.

DASH8-40CW 847 has just crossed the Colorado River and entered Arizona, and is passing a work train laying down new welded rail on October 3, 1997. The back of the train is still in California. The town by the bridge is Topock, which has camping and boating facilities along the Colorado River. Interstate 40 crosses the river along side the railroad bridge, out of sight in the photo.

A change in geography and time finds BNSF DASH8-40CW 842 working an eastbound CSX train up hill, passing under the ex-Western Maryland Salisbury Viaduct west of Meyersdale, Pa. on September 14, 2004. A combination of 12 years of high speed freight service (842 could possibly be approaching the two million mile mark) and weather have faded and pealed the bright red and silver paint applied when built at GE's Erie, Pa. Locomotive assembly buildings in 1992.

A 1990s version of an A-B-B-A locomotive set is GP60M 145, a rebuilt cabless SD45-2, a cabless B30-7A, and a SD40-2 on a westbound train atTopock, Arizon, on July 7, 1994. The trailing Burlington Northern units show the future merger of the two lines isn't far away.

DASH9-44CW 772 is east bound on October 3, 1997 after crossing the Colorado River. By this time, the new 4,400 hp engines coming from GE were still painted in Warbonnet colors but had BNSF nose and side decals.

4,400hp, DASH9-44CW 636 and two 4,135 hp, DASH8-40CW's are on a westbound train 10 miles west of Kingman on April 26, 1995. The low priority train was seen hours earlier near Seligman. Having come only 70 miles in that time, the train must have hit every siding to let the hotter westbound trailer and container trains pass.

Four GE's roll an eastbound train out of the Golden State and onto the massive double track bridge spanning the Colorado River, on April 26, 1995. From here this train will climb out of the Colorado River basin (520') for 214 miles on a 1.4% ruling grade until reaching the summit at the Arizona Divide (7354') west of Flagstaff.

As the four GE's swing past me, they meet the westbound lead by DASH9-44CW 636, which will soon arrive at Needles, California,15 miles away, for a crew change. From there the train will cross the Mojave Desert to Barstow.

As soon as trains depart westbound from Needles, Ca., they encounter 31 miles of 1.4% ruling grade known as Goff's Hill. Here SD40-2 5056 heads west about 10 miles into the grade, on April 23, 1995. By this time, getting a four-unit set all in the old blue and yellow was getting hard to do.

GP60M 134 followed soon after with a trailer train and was running on the eastbound main to go around the lower priority train headed by 5056. The hottest intermodel trains on this line, between Chicago and LA, have a 51-hour schedule, which would mean averaging 43 mph. At first this seems slow, but imagine leaving Chicago in a car and setting your cruise control on 43 mph and not touching it until you reach LA. Now imagine maintaining that schedule on a train, which could be a mile long and 5,000-plus tons.

Earlier in the afternoon, SD40-2 5155 leads another trailer train west. The Santa Fe line roller coasts through the Mojave Desert, with two more summits to cross (Ash Hill, and Lavic) before reaching Barstow, 160 miles to the west.

On April 23, 1995, a new, 4,300 hp SD75M 206 grinds uphill with a heavy westbound double stack train, 10 miles west of Needles. New GM engine orders in the mid-1990s on the Santa Fe were the minority, with GE getting the bigger share of the market with its 4,400 hp, six-axle DASH9-44CW. SD75M's 200-250 had the distinction of being the last new engines delivered in Santa Fe Warbonnet paint. BNSF received 25 more SD75M's in late 1995 through early 1996, in Warbonnet paint, but with BNSF initials.

Over two years later, the line is now BNSF as DASH9-44CW 650 drifts eastbound downhill, at the same location on October 2, 1997. Lighter trailer trains are allowed 60 mph downhill, and the heavier trains 45 mph.

One more shot of Goff's Hill shows DASH8-40CW's 909 and 948 on another westbound trailer train, on October 2, 1997. Eastbound trains can sneak up on you quickly on a windy day. Sometimes the road crossing, a half mile to the west, is the first warning of an approaching train. Westbounds having just started at Needles give you plenty of warning, running wide open, fighting the grade; most trains are at 35mph or under, unless it's the Southwest Chief.

Near the Summit of Goff's Hill (2,500'), a westbound mixed train struggles uphill, on July 6, 1994. GP60 4032 along with a rebuilt cables, six-axle, DASH8-40BW, GP60M and a GP30 have a few more uphill miles to climb, then start on a 43-mile, 1.1% downgrade through Cadiz. The 170 miles between Needles and Barstow, Ca., is known as the Needles Subdivision.

East of Ludlow, California, SD40-2 5100 brings empty container flat cars west, on October 2, 1997. Route 66 cuts off of I-40 at Ludlow and follows the Santa Fe mainline east before it reconnects with I-40 just west of Needles.

DASH8-40BW 530 brings an eastbound trailer train at the same location, on October 2, 1997. In this part of the Mojave Desert, water and vegetation are just a rumor. In steam days, water was hauled in special trains to remote locations to quench the steam engines' never-ending demand. It's little wonder that this was one of the first areas dieselized when the freight FT's from GM started arriving on the Santa Fe in the early 1940s.

Again east of Ludlow, on October 2, 1997, DASH 9-44CW 646 leads another eastbound train. 16,935 GE horsepower effortlessly brings the short, forty-car auto-rack train across the Mojave Desert at 70 mph. In 1936, Santa Fe's premier passenger train was started over this line, 2,222 miles from Chicago to Los Angeles. The Super Chief covered the distance on a 39 ½-hour schedule. The train would have to average 56 mph, including all station stops, train meets, inspections, crew changes, and other variables along the way.

BNSF DASH8 -40CW 869 leads a westbound, double-stack train at Tehachapi, Ca., on September 29, 1997.

An eastbound BNSF trailer train works uphill through the Tehachapi Loop, on September 29, 1997. Tehachapi Loop is located 120 miles north of Los Angeles and just west of the town of Tehachapi. Southern Pacific built south of Sacramento through the San Joaquin Valley to Bakersfield, then in 1876 pushed through the Tehachapi Mountains to the town of Mojave, and on to Los Angeles. The Santa Fe obtained tracking rights over SP from Mojave to Bakersfield in 1900.

Los Angeles-bound trains head southwest from Barstow, while northern California trains head west to Mojave where they pick up Union Pacific's (ex-SP) Tehachapi line to Bakersfield and back to home rails to the San Francisco Bay area. At Mojave (2,745'), the line climbs west to the summit (4,024') just east of the town of Tehachapi and downhill to Bakersfield (414'), on grades as steep as 2.2%. Here an eastbound BNSF train is in the upper part of the loop, on September 30, 1997. From the railhead at the tunnel at the bottom of the loop, to where the rails cross over the top of the tunnel, the grade gains 77' in elevation.

Part of the Mojave Subdivision, the sixty-seven miles of line between Mojave and Bakersfield handles about 40 trains in a 24-hour period, with about half UP and half BNSF. Westbound BNSF DASH8-40CW 869 has double stacks rolling downhill in the late evening, on September 29, 1997. The top of the loop can be seen over the double stacks in the left of the photo.

These three photos show a westbound train making its way through the loop, on October 1, 1997. Here a DASH8-40CW, two SD75M's, and a DASH9-44CW are on a trailer train one-half mile uphill from the loop, which is directly behind me. The train will circle to the left, through short tunnel #10, and will be at the top of the loop. In the second photo, the train continues around the loop and will cross under itself through tunnel #9, out of view at the bottom left of the photo. In the background, the mainline can be seen heading down the valley.

As the train passes through the tunnel, it turns right into an s-curve, with the last photo showing the engines almost through the s-curve. With the front of the train heading west, the back of the train, seen to the left of the photo, momentarily is heading east.

Two DASH9-44CW's are taking ballast cars west as they drop downgrade around the loop, on October 1, 1997. I was somewhat surprised to see two new GE's assigned to the work train. As in the 1930s, the 1990's red, silver, and yellow Warbonnet makes a lasting impression that remains long after the engines were repainted in BNSF colors.

A westbound, BNSF train is about to enter tunnel #10 above the loop, on September 30, 1997. From Caliente east through the loop and on to the town of Tehachapi, this 23 miles of track has a 25-mph speed limit. The heavier trains require helpers, and are mostly cut in at mid-train.

As soon as the train above clears, a Union Pacific train works an eastbound uphill at the same location. Two fallen flags are shown, with two ex-Southern Pacific SD70M's and an ex-Rio Grande tunnel motor on the train. The "Sunset Route" and the railroad that went "Thru The Rockies, Not Around Them" became history with the Union Pacific takeover in 1996.

NW3 181 sits on display beside the Whitefish, Mt., station, on September 20, 1993. 181 were built by GM in 1942; it was basically a switcher on a longer road engine frame and trucks. The extra space was for a steam boiler, so the engines could be used for branch line mixed and passenger train service. GN was the only railroad to acquire the 1000 hp NW3, getting 7 between 1939 and 1942.

I am standing outside the Denver train station, on October 21, 1984, waiting for the eastbound California Zephyr, as Burlington Northern F45 6616 and two U33C's pass by. The Great Northern ordered 14 F45's in 1969, and had twelve more on order for 1970. 6616 was delivered after the merger, and is painted in Burlington Northern cascade green. With the start up of Burlington Northern, 15 ex-Great Northern and 10 ex-Northern Pacific U33C's would be added to their roster. BN would return to GE for 39 more of the 3,300 hp locomotives in 1971, with 5742 and 5755 being part of that order. Twenty more F45's would also be ordered from GM in 1971.

Goat Boat DASH9-44CW 975 waits for a crew on a westbound train at the Whitefish yards, on September18, 1997. When the new 4,400 hp engines started arriving, they were assigned to the old Great Northern route and were delivered in a GN-inspired paint scheme. Too bad a "Rocky the Goat" decal isn't placed under the cab number. If the GN had survived as an independent company, the scene probably would look much the same.

On September 9, 1993, three SD40-2's bring an eastbound train into the yards at Whitefish. From here, the old GN mainline heads west to Spokane, Washington, then continues west over the Cascade Mountains to Everett and down to Seattle. The line also runs north from Everett and connects with Canadian railroads at Vancouver, British Columbia. A line also runs southwest out of Spokane, using the old Northern Pacific line to Pasco. From here, the trains may travel west over Stampede Pass, reopened in the late 1990s to Tacoma, or west along the Columbia River to Portland, Oregon, using the old Spokane, Portland & Seattle Railway that was jointly owned by Great Northern and Northern Pacific.

SD40-2 7087, with two Conrail and two more BN SD40-2's, hauls a westbound grain train downhill, having just passed through West Glacier, on September 20, 1993. West Glacier is the west entrance to Glacier National Park's "Going to the Sun Highway." In 1910, Glacier National Park was created. Great Northern operated the major hotels in the park from 1914 to1960 through its subsidiary, Glacier Park Hotel Company.

Two SD40-2's and a B30-7A haul an eastbound double-stack uphill a half mile east of Essex, Mt., on September 20, 1993. At Essex, at trackside is the Izaak Walton Hotel, which is served by Amtrak's Empire Builder. Built by Great Northern to house train crews and track workers, the hotel was later sold. From here, eastbound trains encounter a 1.8%, 18-mile climb to the Continental Divide at Marias Pass (5,213'), which is the lowest western mainline crossing in the U.S.

Construction of the line was completed in 1892, with the line being built from the west and east simultaneously, joining in the Marias Pass area. Here at Essex, 101 years later, on September 20, 1993, the Empire Builder passes eastbound with three F40PH's, as a SD40-2 sits in the yard with a work train. GN's "See America First" and "Glacier National Park" slogans appeared in 1914 to promote travel to the Pacific Northwest.

The mainline follows the southern boundary of Glacier National Park from West Glacier, 60 miles east to East Glacier. Here, an eastbound train at Java Bridge (10 miles east of Essex) with GP38-2 2150 is on the 1.8%, 18-mile climb to Marias Pass, on September 20, 1993. Westbound trains have a 1% grade of 80 miles to reach the summit. This line is part of the Montana Division.

Amtrak's eastbound Empire Builder passes shortly after the freight train powered by 2150. The name of this daily train isn't new. The Great Northern entered into service a new premier passenger train on a 63-hour schedule, from Chicago to the Pacific Northwest, on June 10, 1929. The train was named in honor of the railroad's founder and first president, James J. Hill, who had acquired the nickname "Empire Builder" from his ability to build the northern-most transcontinental railroad across America and help open-up the Pacific Northwest.

On September 19, 1997, DASH9-44CW's 1037 and 964 head an east-bound, stack train downhill, after cresting the grade at Marias Pass. The old GN mainline heads east to Minot, North Dakota, where one line runs east to Duluth and another line runs on a more southern route through Fargo and onto Minneapolis and St Paul. From St. Paul to Chicago, the old Chicago Burlington and Quincy Railroad, which was owned by Great Northern and Northern Pacific, is used.

Since 1994, around 1,400 of these 4,400 hp, DC traction motor engines have been ordered by BNSF for the higher speed trains. In late 1999, BNSF received a few AC traction motor GE's, which can operate at lower speeds than DC units without damage to the traction motors; they are ideal for heavy coal trains. BNSF depends mostly on GM's SD70MAC's for coal train service, with nearly 800 units placed in service between 1993 and 2000.

Another eastbound train, on September 20, 1997, was in the same location, with two more DASH9-44CW's heading toward East Glacier. GE's FDL Series engines go back to 1959 with the introduction of the U25B, powered by a 2,500 hp FDL16, and continue with the 12-cylinder, 3,200 hp 7 FDL12 and 16-cylinder, 4,400 hp 7FDL16 used in DASH9 and AC models. In 2003, GE came out with their new 12-cylinder 4400 hp. GEVO-12 engines for their new ES44AC and ES44DC locomotives, which are more fuel efficient and produce less emissions.

SD40-2 7846 led a westbound train 10 miles east of the summit, on September 20, 1997. A surprise was the third engine back, Santa Fe GP20 3035. The 2,000 hp unit had been in service for 37 years, far more than GM probably had intended. Santa Fe rebuilt 50 GP20s in the late 1970s to extend their lives, but finding one on a long-haul container train in the late 1990s is rare.

A westbound train drops downhill one mile west of the summit with GP50's 3162, 3125, a leased GM six-axle, a SD40-2, and a B30-7A, on September 19, 1997. Glacier National Park provides the background. The 1970 merger to create Burlington Northern was not a new concept. James J. Hill attempted this consolidation in 1904, but failed. It would take 66 years for his plan to become reality. BN would receive 63 GP50's between 1980 and 1985, with 3162 being the last one delivered. The locomotive is one of five built for the railroad with an extended cab, to accommodate extra crew members with the reduction of cabooses. Shortly after, most trains were reduced down to a two-person crew, making the larger cab unnecessary.

I'm standing at the 5,213' summit as three SD40-2's move westbound stacks past an eastbound stack train, on September 20, 1997. The SD40 and successor SD40-2 have become the all time sales leaders in North America, at the time of this writing. In its production run of twenty two years, from 1966 to the mid-1980s, GM built 5,752 of these six-axle, 3,000 hp locomotives for more than forty railroads throughout the U.S., Canada, and Mexico. They were powered by a 16-645E3C engine, which was introduced in 1966 with the GP38's, and used until 1987 with the upgraded 16-645 F3B used in the SD50s. In 1985, GM's new 12-710G3 engine was introduced in the 3,000 hp, GP59. It was followed by the 16-cylinder version 16-710G3 used in the GP60s and continues to be used in the SD70s.

The Great Northern acquired seventeen GP30's between April and May of 1963. With its new style nose, rounded cab roof, and unique hump from the cab roof to the back of the dynamic brake grid, the GP30 was the most recognizable, second-generation diesel produced by GM. Despite its relatively short production time, from July 1961 to November 1963, 948 of the 2,250 hp engines were built for twenty-seven railroads. The 2,500 hp GP35 replaced the GP30, minus the hump, and a new angled cab roof that wouldn't change until the arrival of the safety cabs. Former Great Northern 3012, now Burlington Northern 2212, heads a work train west past the East Glacier station, on June 14, 1984.

An eastbound, double-stack train leaves the Rocky Mountains behind and starts across Montana's high plains. SD40-2 6926 and B30-7A 4061 have just crossed Two Medicine Bridge, which is 210' high. They are climbing a short grade to Spotted Robe, then down-grade again to Blackfoot, on September 19, 1997.

At the same spot, on September 20, 1997, three DASH9-44CW's, three SD40-2's, and a B30-7A use their combined 25,200 hp to lift a heavy mixed train up the short grade. Burlington Northern received 120 of the cabless B30-7A's from GE in 1982 and 1983. Although the cabless units are less expensive, they aren't as versatile as the standard units and fell out of favor in the 1960s. Santa Fe also ordered cabless engines in the early 1990s with the GP60B's from GM.

The same train that is in the previous photo, taken on September 20, 1997, is shown a few moments before, as it left the Glacier Park area. The Rocky Mountains must have looked like an imposing obstacle to overcome for the track crews after coming from the east, over the plains of North Dakota and Montana. When the line was completed, it was an easier crossing of the Rockies' than Northern Pacific's route to the south, and after the Burlington Northern merger it became the main Chicago-to-the-Pacific Northwest route.

Another eastbound stack train is shown 10 miles west of East Glacier, behind DASH9-44CW 1002 and two SD40-2's, on September 19, 1997. As with other railroads in the 1970s and 1980s, the SD40-2's were BN's most numerous diesel, with 25 SD40s and 746 SD40-2's ordered. But with the hundreds of new GE's and GM's acquired in the 1990s, the locomotive that seemed to be everywhere on the Burlington Northern slowly became less dominate.

The Amtrak Empire Builder is eastbound, having just left East Glacier Station, on September 20, 1997. GE DASH8-P40B's 821 and 800 have replaced the older GM F40PH's that were common a few years previous. The GE's produce 4,000 hp compared to the GM's 3,000 hp, allowing Amtrak to run two instead of three engines on the train. For years, the Great Northern line was BN's first choice for train traffic. The Northern Pacific line through southern Montana had far steeper grades, and BN was looking for a way to close the line. In 1987 the Montana Rail Link Railroad was created, taking over the NP mainline between Jones Junction, east of Billings, Montana, and west 510 miles to Sandpoint, Idaho. Another 94-mile second mainline, between De Smet and Paradise, and 217 miles of branchline was obtained. With rail traffic increases in the 1990s, the mostly single-tracked Great Northern line was at capacity. More BSNF traffic has started to run through again on the old "Main Street of the Northwest" line, which back in the 1980s Burlington Northern was sure was not needed.

An unexpected site as the eastbound Empire Builder rolls into Minot, North Dakota, on May 5, 1982. Amazingly, this wooden water tank had outlasted the steam engine on the GN by 24 years. The late afternoon light reveals a weathered look caused by years of North Dakota summer heat and subzero winters.

Three SD70MAC's have 15,000 tons of Powder River coal moving uphill, 25 miles south of Northport, Nebraska, on September 10,1997. The line is an old Chicago, Burlington and Quincy line that runs north from BNSF's Chicago to Denver line at Brush, Colorado; through Alliance, Nebraska; then west through the southwest corner of South Dakota and northeastern Wyoming; and then into south-central Montana to a connection with the old Northern Pacific mainline at Jones Junction, near Billings.

A few miles to the south, the train had to stop for track crews. Here, 9604 has the train back in motion as it rolls by, in notch 8, at 45 mph. At Sidney the train will cross over Union Pacific's Nebraska mainline, continue to Denver, then run the "Joint Line" to Southern Junction and onto Trinidad, Colorado. From there, the train will head east through northeastern New Mexico and into Texas, to the cities of Fort Worth, Dallas, Houston, or Galveston.

At the same location, on September 27, 1998, new SD70MAC 9897 and five others haul an empty coal train from Texas back to the mines. Three engines are always on the eastbound-loaded trains until they get through Colorado. Two engines are usually enough for the easier grades to the east. As these cut-off units build-up, they are added to the empty trains back to the Powder River area.

Again, the same train is shown, on September 27, 1998. 9897 can't have too many miles behind it, as a side view shows no road grime has built up on the trucks or fuel tank. With the 770-plus SD70MAC's acquired from 1993 through 1999, and more on order, the days are numbered for DC traction-motored SD40-2's and C30-7's on the heavy coal trains.

C30-7 5076 leads a loaded coal train into Alliance, Nebraska, coming north on the line from Northport ,on September 10, 1997. The line north between Colorado and Alliance is known as the Angora Subdivision. At Alliance, the train will take the Sand Hills Subdivision to the east. This line handled around twenty loaded and twenty empty coal trains a day, along with five non-coal trains, in the mid-1990s. The C30-7 was GE's answer to GM's SD40-2. Although not as successful in sales, 1,078 were built by GE between 1976 and 1986.

Well liked by BN, 242 C30-7's were ordered from GE between 1976 and 1981, for heavy coal train service. C30-7 5045, with two more C30-7's and a Kansas City Southern SD60, haul eastbound coal near Edgemont, South Dakota, on September 17, 1998. The train came east from Gillette, Wyoming, on the Black Hills Subdivision and over the Butte Subdivision to Alliance. This line connects with the old Northern Pacific mainline east of Billings, Montana, and runs southeast through Gillette, Alliance, and on to Lincoln, Nebraska.

DASH9-44CW 4736 is on an eastbound train at Fairmont, Nebraska, 40 miles west of Lincoln, on October 1, 1998, along the old Chicago, Burlington & Quincy Denver to Chicago mainline. Warbonnet DASH9-44CW 718, SD40-2 6915, and F45 6966 help power the mixed train, which has 30 flat cars of concrete ties on the head end for track improvements to the east. The last engine is ex- Rio Grande SD45 5335, dead in tow. The hood was removed over 5335's V-20 engine and hand railings were cut away, which more than likely means that, after 30 years of service, the SD45 is heading east for the last time to the scrapers.

The Sand Hills Subdivision runs from Lincoln, Nebraska, west to Alliance. On September 10, 1997, two Oakway SD60s and a UP DASH8-40C are 20 miles east of Alliance with a loaded train. Burlington Northern leased 100 SD60s through Oakway Inc., which are maintained by EMD. By the end of the 1990s, other railroads were starting to do the same, with GE and GM setting up programs to maintain the locomotives, often in the railroads' existing shops.

Trains average 110 to 130 cars, with the longer trains grossing 18,000 tons. Near the same location on the same day, SD60M 9224, SD40-2 7227, and an Oakway SD60 have another eastbound in tow, having just passed an empty train headed for Alliance. The SD60s received GM's new V-16 710 (710 cubic inch per cylinder) engine which produces 3,800 hp. Shortly after, enough SD70MAC's were received from GM, and the DC tractioned SD60M's were sent south to work on the ex-Santa Fe's Chicago to California mainline.

Four C30-7's and an Oakway SD60 are on the head end of a loaded coal train about 6 miles into the climb up 13-mile, 1.55% grade Crawford Hill, on September 28, 1998. All loaded eastbounds pick up helpers at Crawford for the climb to Belmont, which is located 44 miles west of Alliance on the Butte Subdivision. Although the Burlington's slogan, "Everywhere West," was slightly over-exaggerated, the Chicago-based railroad reached west to Wyoming and Montana, and through Colorado to Texas, with its subsidiaries Colorado & Southern, and Fort Worth & Denver Railways.

Three sets of helpers are based out of Crawford. Here a set in the form of four SD40-2's shove the coal train by C30-7 5010. Extra fuel is carried in the tank car splicing the engines. In the mid-90s, two SD70MAC's per set were tried, but the SD40-2's have returned. Even with 144 cylinders cranking out 27,800 horsepower to produce electricity for 54 traction motors, these nine GE's and GM's still have their work cut out for them, as they grind uphill running full throttle at around 10 mph. with the 15,000-plus ton coal train.

Oakway SD60 9001 leads an empty coal train past two crewless trains 14 miles east of Gillette, Wyoming, on September 18, 1998. The train has three possible routes. (1) The train might head south at the junction at Donkey Creek and take the Orin Subdivision. (2) It may go a few miles west to Campbell, where a branch line heads north 10 miles and serves six mines. (3) It may go through Gillette and the mines to the west.

SD70MAC's 9845 and 9963 are set with a loaded train north of Bill, Wyoming, on the Orin Subdivision, on September 18, 1998. The switch to AC traction motors to the locomotives in the 1990s was for several reasons. AC's have a higher adhesion to the rail, are simpler in construction (no brushes and commutators), are less likely to slip, and can obtain long lower speeds without overheating They are ideal for heavy coal train service.

The 127-mile Orin Subdivision is a young railroad. In 1972, Burlington Northern built south from Donkey Creek for 15 miles to the Belle Ayr mine. By 1979, the line was built south to Bridger Junction, where it connected with the former C.B. &Q. Casper, Wyoming, to Northport, Nebraska, line. BNSF and U.P. had 50 loaded and 50 empty coal trains operating daily over the line by the late 1990s. Here, on September 18, 1998, three BNSF SD70MAC's leave the Bill yard with a loaded southbound train.

Three BNSF SD70MAC's have come west on the Sand Hills Subdivision to Alliance, and turned south to Northport for reloading, on September 27, 1998. In the early 1970s, tougher pollution laws caused power plants to switch from eastern coal to the Powder River coal, which burns cleaner because of its lower sulfur content. In 1972, only 30,000 tons were hauled out of the Powder River region, but by 1996 that figure had grown to 250 million tons per year.

Chapter 2
Conrail, Norfolk Southern

By the early 1970s, the railroads of the northeast were in financial trouble, with many in bankruptcy, the system was close to collapse. Unlike the western railroads with long hauls, the eastern lines relied on shorter hauls. With the densely populated areas along the east coast, the highway and interstate road building starting in the 1950s paralleled many of the rail lines. The trucking industry drained away traffic that the smaller railroads and some large railroads would never recover. On February 5, 1976, President Ford signed the Railroad Revitalization and Regulatory Act, which made available $6.4 billion dollars for Conrail, Amtrak's Northeast Corridor, and commuter lines, plus gave the railroads some control on setting their own rates. On April 1, 1976, the government resumed control of Penn Central, Erie Lackawanna, Lehigh Valley, Reading, Central Railroad of New Jersey, Lehigh & Hudson River, and Pennsylvania-Reading Seashore Lines, to form Conrail. The government was now in charge of a 17,000-mile rail system that would require huge sums of money to get it back in shape. Conrail had many doubters about the railroad's chances of survival, but by the early 1980s the railroad showed its first profit. On October 21, 1986, President Reagan signed a bill that allowed the sale of Conrail. On March 25, 1987, Conrail's stock went public. On June 1, 1999, Conrail was split between Norfolk Southern (58%) and CSX (42%). Although Conrail lasted only from 1976 to 1999, its 23 years had a huge impact on making the northeast rail system once again an important transportation link.

Still with their original Pennsy road numbers, SD45's 6191 and 6125 push a westbound trailer train around Horseshoe Curve on May 24, 1980. The Pennsylvania Railroad received 130 SD45's from EMD between October 1966 and January 1968.

Two Norfolk Southern SD70M's bring an eastbound train into Altoona, Pa., on May 10, 2003. To meet with EPA emission standards for new engines, GM would modify the SD70M's with larger radiators and cooling systems, going back to the SD45-styled flared radiators. In the early 1980s, GM would redesign the dynamic brake equipment, doing away with a dynamic brake blister bulge on the top middle of the long hood, and giving these new engines a sort of Chicago & North Western look.

These two photos are taken along the ex-New York Central New York to Chicago mainline just east of North East, Pennsylvania on September 30, 1982. At one time this was a four track mainline which saw the passage of NYC's famous 4-6-4 Hudson's, and the 20th Century Limited. Above: SD40 6262 hits a low spot on the eastbound main. Below; another eastbound later in the day powered by SD40 6333 and two newer SD40-2's. By the late 1990s, up to 70 freight trains and Amtrak's Lake Shore Limited used this route every day. With the split of Conrail on June 1, 1999, this ex- NYC line was taken over by CSX.

Conrail U25B 2624 and a GP38 power a westbound train at Ludlow, Pa. in November of 1981, on the ex-Pennsylvania Railroad Erie to Emporium line. The U25B was GE's first successful road engine, with 478 built between 1959 and 1966. At 2,500 hp., they jumped ahead of EMD and ALCO in the horsepower race. It would take EMD until 1963 to come out with the 2,500 hp. GP35, and ALCO also in 1963 with the six-axle, 2,750 hp. C628 to catch GE. 2624 was one of 59 built for Pennsylvania Railroad between 1962 and 1965. Conrail would acquire the largest fleet of the model with 179. In four months, 2624's 20 years of service would come to an end in a derailment on March 25, 1982, south of Utica, New York.

The Horseshoe Curve is located 6 miles west of Altoona, Pa. on the ex-Pennsylvania Railroad's Pittsburgh Region. It opened to traffic with a single track on February 15, 1854. From Altoona, westbounds have a 1.8 % climb for the twelve miles to Gallitzin, then a 1.05 % downgrade of 27 miles to Johnstown. Fourteen helper sets are used between Johnstown and Altoona. Here at the Horseshoe Curve, on May 23, 1980, two SD45's are the helpers on a westbound trailer train. 6191 and 6125 were part of an order of SD45's that turned out to be Pennsy's last locomotive order.

In June 1981, SD40-2 6508 rolls around the Curve westbound without helpers. The weight of the train was too much for a Chicago and North Western boxcar located behind the gondolas, which pulled a coupler in two when it passed me. The outside track was out of service for 1 ½ hours until repairs were made. Helpers were placed on the back to get the heavy train started.

Another westbound passes the park at Horseshoe Curve, on July 26, 1980. SD40-2 6364 leads an ex-Erie Lackawanna SD45 and two ex-Penn Central GP38-2's still in their previous owner's colors. With almost 5,000 locomotives acquired in the 1976 startup of Conrail, engines would run for years before getting painted, and many retired before ever receiving Conrail Blue.

Ex-Penn Central SD40 6270 and a SD45 haul a westbound train at the Curve on July 26, 1980. As the older engineer passes by, one can't help but wonder at the changes he must have seen in his railroad career, probably starting out on the Pennsy in the 1940s when the railroad was at the top. The railroad's fortunes would begin to slip in the 1950s through the 1960s. The interstate highway and airline systems, higher taxes, industries relocating to the south and west, and the increase of imported steel would drain away tonnage and passengers from the railroad. The ill-fated merger with New York Central, on February 1, 1968, to create Penn Central would end in bankruptcy in the early 1970s. Conrail's creation in 1976 would slowly start to rebuild the northeast rail system.

Walking across the tracks from the park and up a bank provides this shot of a westbound trailer train and an eastbound coal train, on May 24, 1980. The third engine back on the coal train, a U25B, would be off Conrail's roster by 1982, but its success helped GE to overtake GM in the late 1980s to become the leading locomotive builder in the 1990s.

SD40-2 6449 and 6500 are helpers on a westbound train at the Curve, on April 25, 1981. The number 2 eastbound main had just been taken up. Part of Conrail's cost-cutting efforts in the early 1980s included making the once-four-track railroad across Pennsylvania a three-track line. Pennsy's premier passenger train, The Broadway Limited, received its name not from the famous street in New York City but this former four-track broadway across the Keystone State.

Two SD45's shove a westbound train one mile above the Curve, on September 13, 1980. The helpers stay on the train to Cresson, about three miles past Gallitzin, or, if the train is heavy, will stay on the train for the downhill run to Johnstown to help with braking. Conrail used its older power for helpers, as in this case; if the fuel-hungry V-20 645E engines in the SD45's do breakdown, they are close to Altoona's Juniata Shops.

GP40 3245 leads a westbound trailer train at the lower part of Horseshoe Curve, on April 18, 1981. Within a few years, double stack trains would gain importance, and by the mid-1990s, Conrail would be forced to raise the height of the tunnels at Gallitzin to handle these trains that had previously been sent over longer routes.

Ex-Penn Central 3,300 hp. U33B 2925 heads east with a work train above the Curve, on September 13, 1980. Penn Central received 81 U33B's from GE between 1968 and 1970, and had two that were previously owned by New York Central. The recession in the early 1980s caused these engines to be taken out of service by the mid-80s.

1.5 miles below the Curve, in October 1981, finds the mainline as busy as it can get. Two westbounds are moving uphill as an easbound coal train heads for Altoona. The speed limit from Altoona to Gallitzin is 35 mph for both freight and passenger trains, with coal trains sometimes getting two sets of helpers into Altoona for braking.

SD45-2's 6661 and 6660 help a westbound trailer train at the center of the Horseshoe Curve, in April of 1986. Erie Lackawanna received 13 SD45-2's in 1972 for their New York to Chicago trailer trains. They had the same V-20, 3,600 hp. engine as the SD45, but lack the V-shaped radiators. They were equipped with a 5,000 gallon fuel tank so they could run through on the Erie Lackawanna without refueling.

SD40-2 6490 and ex-Pennsy SD45 6141 bring truck frames and trailers westbound around Horseshoe Curve, on April 25, 1981. 6141 has put in almost 15 years of road service for the Pennsylvania, Penn Central, and Conrail, being built in late 1966. 6490 is one of 42 SD40-2's built for Conrail in 1979.

Ignoring the Conrail Blue on SD40-2 6418 and GP40-2 3299, what more could represent the late Pennsylvania-Penn Central era than black ex-Pennsy SD45 6196 and ex-Penn Central GP38-2's 8146, 8144 bringing a westbound around the four-track mainline at Horseshoe Curve, in August 1980?

GP38-2 8100 brings an eastbound train around Scotch Run Curve, on September 13, 1980. The trailing SD45's 3,600 hp. is only 400 less than the combined 4,000 hp. of the two GP38-2's. This view gives a good comparison of the SD45's' wide-angled hood (to accommodate the larger radiators) with the narrow hoods of the GP38-2's.

GP40-2 3333 (the "four threes"), GP40-2 3280, and GP40 3005 move westbound with truck frames and trailers and are about to enter the lower end of Horseshoe Curve, on April 25, 1987. One of Altoona's water reservoirs can be seen behind the engines.

Two SD45-2's are at the head end of a westbound trailer train about to enter the lower part of Horseshoe Curve, on April 25, 1987.

Anyone with an interest in SD40-2's has to put Altoona on the top of their places to visit. Five SD40-2's bring a eastbound coal train into town, on September 14, 2002. Three more are on the back of the train for braking, plus two can be seen shoving a westbound train in the background. With all the Conrail blue, there is little evidence of the Norfolk Southern buyout over three years before.

Two ex-Conrail SD40-2 helpers are on the end of an eastbound train coming into Altoona, on October 6, 2001. 3333's long front porch would be an ideal place to put a lawn chair for a ride down the mountain.

GP15-1's 1619, 1607, 1624 and GP38 7933 bring a trailer train westbound below the Horseshoe Curve, on April 25, 1987. In the 1970s and 1980s, many railroads were rebuilding their older lower horsepower locomotives. In an attempt to gain some of the market, GM would offer the GP15-1, which used rebuilt components from trade-in locomotives, resulting in a lower cost. Sales were slow with only 368 built, including the GP15AC and GP15T models, between 1976 and 1983. Conrail received 100 of the locomotives in 1979, lacking dynamic brakes and equipped with a non-turbocharged, 12-cylinder 645E rated at 1,500 hp.

The two trailer trains pace each other as they enter the lower portion of the curve. In a little over a mile, the locomotives will be on the far side of the valley, and will have gained 122 feet in elevation.

SD40-2 helpers 6465 and 6473 are cut in ahead of four GP40-2's, using their combined 18,000 hp. to bring a heavy trailer train up-grade, rounding Scotch Run Curve, on September 15, 1981.

SD40 6343 leads a westbound trailer train with truck frames stacked on the lead cars in September 1980, two miles below the Horseshoe Curve. From New York City the ex-Pennsy line runs to Philadelphia and across Pennsylvania to Pittsburgh. From here, the line splits for Chicago and Saint Louis. In the late 1990s, 50 freight and 6 passenger trains a day used this route.

Two C30-7A's shove a westbound train two miles below the Horseshoe Curve, on April 25, 1987. Conrail was the only railroad to purchase this model, with 50 delivered in the spring of 1984. The C30-7A uses a 12-cylinder 7FDL12 instead of the 16-cylinder 7FDL16's used in the C30-7's. Both models are rated at 3,000 hp.

The same location as the above finds eight GE and GM engines on a westbound, 130-car train, on April 18, 1981. The I-beam is attached to the end flat cars, with the center car serving as a spacer. The train is moving slower than normal on account of the oversized load.

There has been a park for train watchers at the Horseshoe Curve since 1879. K4s 1361 (built in 1918 at the Juniata Shops) was put on display in June 1957, to honor the people who built and maintained the Pennsylvania Railroad in the Altoona area. 1361 was pulled from the park in 1985 and restored to service. Ex-Pennsy GP9 7048 replaced the 4-6-2 at the park. In 1992 the park was rebuilt with a gift shop and museum below, and an incline built to reach trackside. It is operated by the Railroaders Memorial Museum of Altoona. To the left, on April 25, 1987, SD40 6289 and SD45-2 6655 shove a westbound uphill, two miles below the curve. Eight car lengths ahead is another westbound train.

On May 23, 1980, the tracks outside the Juniata Shops is filled with a mix of GM diesels awaiting repairs. Repair facilities have existed in Altoona since 1850 for locomotives and cars. The first new locomotive was constructed in the Altoona Shops in November 1866, 4-4-0 142. By the time Pennsy built its last engine here (T1 4-4-4-4 5524) on June 14, 1946, 6873 steam and electric locomotives had been built. For Pennsy, Penn Central, Conrail, and now Norfolk Southern, these shops have been, and are, a major rebuild shop for diesels. In the 1990s new engines were rolling out of Juniata again, as GM and GE couldn't keep up with orders and sent the locomotives in kit form for Juniata to assemble.

In late September 1979, SD40 6264 heads west through Altoona with thirteen engines. Power tends to build up at Harrisburg and occasionally a group of engines will be sent west to Pittsburgh. Altoona was created in 1849 to serve the Pennsylvania Railroad. By the 1920s, over 11,000 employees worked in the machine shops, car shops, engine house, and the Juniata Shops. Also with the train crews and track workers added to the list, one can see why Altoona was truly a railroad town.

On October 3,1998, SD60M 5537 and a SD45-2 bring an eastbound coal train through Altoona. In eight months, change took place in Altoona as black diesels reappeared, but this time in the form of the Norfolk Southern Thoroughbred. Norfolk Southern Corporation was created on June 1, 1982, with the merger of the Norfolk & Western Railway with the Southern Railway.

On September 12, 2000, NS DASH9-40CW 9298 and high hood SD40-2 3325 bring a ballast train eastbound through town. Above the train is the covered walkway to the new combined Amtrak and Bus station. The large building is the Station Shopping Mall. Part of Altoona Railroaders Memorial Museums equipment can be seen. A mix of passenger and freight cars, along with GG1 4913, Baldwin V0660, EMD SW9, and a Pennsy N5c caboose appear above the cab of the GE.

NS SD70 2578, with two high hood GP38's, and Montana Rail Link SD45 316 take an eastbound train through Cresson, on September 12, 2000. Most helpers cut off of westbounds here, and a set can be seen on the left side of 2578. To the right and out of site is a sanding and fueling facility and a building for light repairs. N & W and Southern were buying high-short-hood GE's and GM's into the early 1980s. The other railroads had switched by the early 1960s to the design that cut the short hood down, giving train crews better visibility.

With "Big Blue" split on June 1, 1999, Norfolk Southern took control of mostly former Pennsy lines and CSX took mostly N.Y.C. lines. The ex-Conrail engines have PRR decals under the engine's numbers on the cab to show NS ownership. So, 30 years after its demise, the Pennsy name lives on. To the left, a Norfolk Southern SD40-2 heads an eastbound train into Allegheny Tunnel at Gallitzin, on September 22, 1999.

At 2192 feet in elevation, the rails will drop a little over 1000 feet to Altoona in twelve miles. The next two photos, taken on September 13, 2000, show two westbound trains at Allegheny Tunnel. NS DASH9-40-CW 9413 leads a train made up of gondolas with steel. The heavy train has two sets of SD40-2 helpers, which will probably stay with the train to Johnstown. Allegheny Tunnel was completed in 1854 and Gallitzin Tunnel, to the left, in 1904. Both are 3605 feet in length. Just to the east is the 1,629-foot New Portage Tunnel, built in 1855, which handles most eastbound trains. The New Portage Railroad was built by the state of Pennsylvania to replace the Allegheny Portage Railroad, which operated a system of incline planes to get over the mountains. PRR took control of this line in 1857. This tunnel is slightly higher in elevation than the other two, and trains face a two-mile descent of 2.27% to Benny.

In the early 1960s, Allegheny and New Portage tunnels were single tracked with rails centered in the tunnel to allow high cube boxcars and auto-racks to clear. Double stack trains started running on September 7, 1995, when the clearances were finally completed on Allegheny and New Portage Tunnels. Allegheny Tunnel also reverted back to double track and Gallitzin Tunnel was taken out of service, but will be put back if traffic levels pick up. Although the names have changed, this route across Pennsylvania is still doing what it was designed to do 150 years ago: moving freight 24 hours a day, 7 days a week, 365 days a year between the east coast and mid-west.

Back to Conrail days finds ex-Pennsy GP7 5855 and RS3m 9932 moving eastbound at Altoona, on July 24, 1981. The Pennsylvania would acquire 66 GP7's from 1952 through 1953: 56 for freight and 10 for passenger service. 5855 arrived on the railroad in 1952 for freight service, working along with the last of Pennsy steam, plus just about every diesel model available from GM, ALCO, Baldwin, Fairbanks-Morse, Lima, and General Electric. At nearly 30 years of age, 5855 isn't a good candidate for a new coat of Conrail Blue.

Penn Central would begin a rebuild program to extend the life of their RS3's in 1972 that continued into the Conrail era. The ALCO's 12 cylinder 244D 1600 hp. engine would be removed and replaced with a 12-cylinder, 567B 1200 hp. engine from retired E-Units. Both the ex-New York Central Dewitt Shops at Syracuse, NY, and Juniata Shops at Altoona, Pa. would rebuild the locomotives. Other than the bulge along the top of the long hood, "DeWitt Geep" 9932 retains its ALCO looks, if not its ALCO sounds.

On the same day, a half mile to the east, two more RS3m's, 9929 and 9937, rest in the Altoona Yard. The locomotives would retain their ALCO radiators, but the large, single, cooling fan at the top front of the long hood would be replaced by smaller, twin, EMD cooling fans. With the early 1980s recession and Conrail's desire to rid its roster of older minority power, these locomotives' days were numbered. In the background are boxcars still lettered for Pennsy and New York Central.

C30-7 6608 rests at Juniata Shops with SD40 6261, SW1500 9513, and SW1200 9364, on July 24, 1981. 6608 was from a group of ten conventional 16-cylinder C30-7's that Conrail received in November 1977. The star in front of the road number, under the cab window, indicates a test unit. Conrail would test the costs between the C30-7's and SD40-2's; by 1980 the results showed GM engines had the advantage. The railroad would favor GM in the 1980s, but by the early 1990s GE sales would predominate.

Norfolk Southern GP40 1384 is eastbound, with a Jordan Spreader and bay window caboose, near North East, Pa., on September 30, 1982. The train is on the former Nickel Plate Road mainline to Buffalo, N.Y. Conrail's ex-N.Y.C. mainline can be seen in the right of the photo, which would go to CSX in the 1999 Conrail split. 1384 was one of 29 GP40s built for Norfolk & Western between 1966 and 1967. By the merger with Southern, N & W operated around 7500 miles of track.

SD40-2 3325 is eastbound on a ballast train at Altoona, on September 12, 2000. 3325 was built in 1979 for Southern subsidiary Central of Georgia Railway, which the railroad acquired in 1963. Before its merger with Norfolk and Western in 1982, the Southern was a 10,250-mile, thirteen-state system. With Norfolk Southern rebuilding its high nose GP38's into low nose GP38-2's, chances are its only a matter of time before 3325 will lose its unique high short hood. As with N & W and Southern, new Norfolk Southern engines through the mid-1980s were set up to run long hood forward.

By 2005 Norfolk Southern had 1023 DASH9-40CW's on their roster. Most trains through Altoona, by 2005, were averaging 62 per day and seemed to be powered by the 4000 hp. GE's, as the next three photos show. 9406 brings an eastbound off the hill as it rolls into the west end of Altoona, on October 6, 2001.

9397 brings double stacks westbound as it overtakes another westbound, mixed freight departing Altoona, on October 6, 2001.

9293 is westbound with a slab steel train at Altoona, on September 14, 2002. These heavy trains of 90 to 100 gondolas rate four or five SD40-2's for a push up the hill. Occasionally a second section of the steel train will follow.

About five miles west of Cresson is the town of Cassandra. An old bridge provides a good view of the mainline, on May 25, 2004. SD70M 2597 and DASH9-40CW 9753 are about to pass under the bridge westbound, with a double-stack train. DASH8-40CW 8347 and DASH9-40CW 9573 work uphill with an eastbound mixed train.

On August 17, 2001, I was looking at some old slides with my sister that my Dad had taken in Sheffield, Pa. in the early 1960s, with Pennsy's Erie-to-Emporium line in the background. I had thought to myself, I wish Dad had taken a photo of a freight train, or better yet the 580 eastbound Erie-to-Emporium, or 581 westbound Emporium-to-Erie passenger train powered by an E8. Passenger service ended on this line March 27, 1965. Amazingly, the headline in the local paper the following day announced that ex-Pennsylvania Railroad passenger locomotives would operate over this line on a three-day, Philadelphia-Conneaut, Ohio-Pittsburgh- Philadelphia round trip, with a private passenger car train, on August 19. Rain on Sunday morning would slowly end, and at around 1:30 in the afternoon, a mile east of Ludlow, the Pennsy era would return briefly as E8's 5711 and 5809 are westbound with the train. Pennsy's E8's and earlier passenger engines were delivered in Brunswick Green, with five gold pin-stripes starting at the nose and running along the side of the locomotive. By the end of 1952, colors were changed to Tuscan Red with five gold stripes. 5711 and 5809 represent the late 1950s and early 1960s, when the railroad went to the single, broad, gold stripe. Not showing any signs of their nearly 50 years of age, the ex-Pennsy locomotives make a impressive site as they pass the Route 6, Dorcon Road Crossing at Warren.

Ex-Chicago, Burlington & Quincy #377, the Silver Solarium from the California Zephyr, was a part of the train and is shown running in reverse at Weldbank. The California Zephyr was a joint effort between the C. B. & Q., Rio Grande, and the Western Pacific, operating 2532 miles between Chicago and San Francisco. Known for its multi-dome cars, the train was scheduled to pass through WP's Feather River Canyon, and Rio Grande's crossing of the Rockies in daylight hours. Service began on March 20, 1949, but as with other long distance passenger trains, the airlines and interstate highways took their toll, and after 21 years the CZ would make its last run on March 22, 1970. The Vista-Dome observation car was built by Budd in 1948 and was one of 78 cars built for the train. To provide daily east and westbound service, six train sets had to be operated.

Chapter 3
CSX Transportation

CSX Corporation was formed on November 1, 1980, when Chessie System and Seaboard Coast Line were merged, but they maintained their separate identities. Chessie System was created on February 26, 1973, with the merges of the Baltimore & Ohio, Chesapeake & Ohio, and the Western Maryland, to create an 11,140-mile railroad. Seaboard Coast Line was created on July 1, 1967, with the merger of the Seaboard Air Line and the Atlantic Coast Line. On December 29, 1982, the Louisville & Nashville Railroad was added to the SCL to create the Seaboard System Railroad. The Clinchfield Railroad, Georgia Railroad, Western Railway of Alabama, Atlanta & West Point Railroad, and the Newberry & Laurens Railroad were acquired by Seaboard System, creating a 15,400-mile railroad. CSX Corporation was involved in many industries besides the railroad. In 1985 it divided itself into four divisions: Transportation, Technology, Energy, and Properties. The railroad division was renamed CSX Transportation. Finally, on August 31, 1987, Chessie System and Seaboard System were officially merged to operate as one system, the 26,000-mile CSXT. On June 1, 1999, Conrail was divided up between Norfolk Southern and CSX. CSX gained 42 percent of Conrail, bringing the total miles of track to 33,000. By the end of the 1990s, the United States would have only two major rail systems in the east and two in the west.

B. & O. GP9 6510 hauls a northbound coal train uphill at Watson Farm, in July of 1978, on the Knox, Pa.-to-Mt. Jewett, Pa. branchline. The B. & O. acquired a sizeable fleet of Geeps in the 1950s, with 32 GP7's, 193 GP9's, and a single GP18 in 1962.

Even though the Baltimore & Ohio name officially disappeared in 1987, it's still possible to see remnants of the "Capital Dome Route," as seen here on the back of a cast iron whistle sign two miles north of Watson Farm, Pa., on March 24, 2003.

A southbound, Buffalo and Pittsburgh train is three miles north of Mt. Jewett, Pa., on September 25, 1988. When the B&P took over operations on the former B&O Buffalo Division, in July of 1988, they leased CSX engines until they could acquire their own. Ex-B&O GP40 6637 is followed by four more CSX engines and a B&P GP9.

CSX AC4400CW 158 brings a freight eastbound, descending the Sand Patch Grade six miles west of Cumberland, Md., on May 15, 1996. The ex-Baltimore and Ohio mainline comes west from Baltimore and Washington to Cumberland, where a line continues west to the West Virginia coal fields. At one time it reached St. Louis. Another line heads northwest up Sand Patch Grade to Pittsburgh and continues west to Chicago. This line sees about 30 freights and Amtrak's east and westbound, Chicago to Washington Capital Limited, daily.

At the Summit of Sand Patch Grade, on September 23,1999, an eastbound coal train, with ex-Conrail SD80-MAC 808 and a CSX SD70 MAC, is about to pass the highest point on the line at 2,258'. A few thousand feet ahead, the train will enter the 4475' Sand Patch Tunnel, completed in 1913 to replaced the 4,777' original, single-track tunnel that opened to traffic in 1871. The southern route to St Louis opened up through Cumberland in the 1840s, with the line to Pittsburgh opened in 1871. The SD80MAC is powered by a 20-710G3B-ES engine that produces 5000 hp., which is the first V-20 produced by GM since its V-20 645E's used in SD45's from the mid-1960s to mid-1970s. Conrail was the only railroad to order this model from GM, buying 30 between 1995 and 1996. With the Conrail split, CSX received 13 and Norfolk Southern got 17 of these AC engines.

I'm standing on the old Western Maryland Salisbury Viaduct, which crosses over the CSX line just west of Meyersdale, Pa., on September 11, 2000. WM ran from Baltimore, Md. with lines to York, Pa. and Shippensburg, Pa., across Maryland to Cumberland. From here, lines ran to Elkins, W.V., and on to Webster Springs. The line from Cumberland to Connellsville, Pa., opened to traffic in 1912. With the WM consolidated into Chessie System in 1973, much of the WM was soon abandoned. Traffic moved over to the B&O lines that paralleled most of its routes. With the line to Connellsville taken out of service, the only traffic the 1908'-long, 101'-high Salisbury Viaduct sees today is people, who now use the bridge on the newly opened hike-bike trail.

The CSX DASH8-44CW #9015 leads a westbound trailer train downhill, about to pass under the viaduct, and DASH9-P42B 24 leads the eastbound Capital Limited. GE built 121 of these 4200 hp. engines for Amtrak between 1996 and 1997. Eastbound trains between Connellsville and Sand Patch summit climb 960 feet in 59 miles, with a 1.2 percent ruling grade, while the westbound trains face a tougher climb. From Cumberland to Sand Patch summit, the rails climb 1620 feet in 33 miles, with a 1.8 percent ruling grade. Helpers work both sides of the hill using mostly SD50s. The 92 miles between Cumberland and Connellsville is the former B & O's Main Line Subdivision.

A lightning storm would chase me off Salisbury Viaduct, on May 9, 2003. As I reached my truck, an eastbound train could be heard. A half mile east of the viaduct, tie replacement is in progress as AC4400 CW 88 brings the train uphill at reduced speed.

Another photo from Salisbury Viaduct. DASH8-40C 7615 leads an eastbound container train, on May 25, 2005. The eastbound track was out of service for rail replacement, so all trains were running on the westbound main. Splicing the two DASH8-40C's, the 212-ton AC6000CW's 76-foot length, 5500-gallon fuel tank, and oversized radiators are quite apparent.

After assisting an eastbound train to Sand Patch Summit, SD50's 8545 and 8502 drift downhill westbound, on September 14, 2004. Both locomotives were built for Seaboard System, 8502 in 1983 and 8545 in 1984.

Again at the top of Sand Patch Grade, on September 13, 2002, CSX GE AC6000CW 626 leads a westbound mixed train about to pass the crest of the summit of the Alleghenies at 2258'. CSX had at this time acquired the largest fleet of the 6000 hp. engines, with a total of 117.

The only drawback to Saalisbury Viaduct is that old Route 219 and the new Route 219 bypass around Meyersdale pass under the viaduct. The constant noise from vehicles makes it tough to hear approaching trains. Westbounds give a few minutes warning with numerous grade crossings in Meyersdale. With eastbounds, the first indication of them many times is moments before they reach the grade crossing west of the viaduct. On September 16, 2004, (ex-Conrail 6744) SD50 8662, in fresh CSX colors, and C30-7 7054 bring a mixed freight eastbound.

The line west to Cumberland, Md., would be complete by late 1842. The B&O would follow the West Virginia side of the Potomac River, winding 16 miles between Paw Paw and east to Orleans Road, which was 8 air miles away. The Western Maryland Railway would open a parallel route through here in 1903, giving the B&O a reason to build the Magnolia Cutoff in 1913-1914. Two miles west of Paw Paw, the new double-track line would run east using four tunnels and two large bridges, and rejoining the old mainline at Orleans Road, cutting the distance roughly in half. The old mainline was used for passenger and occasional freight trains until 1961. On September 9, 2003, SD70MAC 8736 is east of Paw Paw crossing over the Potomac River and rolling into West Virginia on the Magnolia Bridge with an eastbound train. The 1592-foot Graham Tunnel in Maryland is in the background. On the other side of the tunnel is the Kessler Bridge crossing again over the Potomac River, with the back of the train, as with the front, in West Virginia.

Later in the day, DASH8-40CW 7813 has an eastbound autorack train at the same location.

Just east of the bridge on the same day, AC4400 CW 17 splits the double color position light signals at 50 mph with a westbound trailer train.

The B&O reached Harpers Ferry, West Virginia, in 1834. Because of the town's location near the divided North and South, its arsenal production, and the B&O mainline, the town was hit hard by the Civil War. On September 10, 2002, SD70MAC's 8735 and 8749 bring a westbound trailer train into Harpers Ferry. In the background is the 925' Harpers Ferry Tunnel in Maryland, and the 1,376' bridge bringing the railroad across the Potomac River.

AC6000CW 5013 has an eastbound train crossing the Potomac River at Harpers Ferry, on September 10, 2002. I'm standing on the former mainline bridge, built in 1894, now used as a walkway and by CSX to reach Strasburg, Virginia, 50 miles to the south. This line is the B & O's old Shenandoah Subdivision. Originally the Winchester and Potomac Railroad, the line leaves the mainline at Harpers Ferry Tunnel and follows the Shenandoah River. The bridge in the foreground was completed in 1931, along with the widening of the west end of Harpers Ferry Tunnel. The East End Subdivision of the Cumberland Division runs 94 miles from Cumberland east through Harpers Ferry and on to Weverton, Maryland.

Roughly half-way between Harpers Ferry and Cumberland is the small yard of Hancock, West Virginia, on the ex-B&O mainline. From here, a six-mile branchline ran to Berkeley Springs, WV. The line provided the B&O revenue with as many as 14,000 carloads of glass sand a year. About two miles of the branchline is still in service to reach the U.S. Silica sand mine. Four miles west of Hancock, AC6000CW 652 and a mix of nine more GE's and GM's, with a combined horsepower of over 40,000, bring a heavy mixed train uphill westbound, winding along the West Virginia side of the Potomac River, on September 10, 2003. How long the steam era B&O color position light signals will survive is anybody's guess.

After AC6000 CW 652 had passed, the westbound track was taken out of service for track maintenance. Heavy AC4400 CW 5115 and a SD70MAC run west on the eastbound track. I'm standing on what, at one time, was the third track.

Two miles west of Hancock in the early morning of September 10, 2003, the sunlight hasn't reached the valley along the Potomac River as SD50 8526 smokes through with a westbound train.

Shortly after the westbound passed, SD70MAC 8743 shows with an eastbound. CSX would go to GM for A.C. power and acquire 90 SD70MAC's between 1997 and 2002. By comparison, GE A.C. orders totaled 711. CSX wasn't an isolated case. By 2004, GE was building four locomotives for every one GM built. In early 2005, General Motors would sell its Electro-Motive Division to Greenbriar Equity Group LLC and Berkshire Partners LLC. After 70 plus years and over 58,000 locomotives, GM would be out of the railroad business.

Chapter 4
Union Pacific Railroad

The Union Pacific has the distinction of being the only major railroad in the United States to retain its original name, created by the Pacific Rail Act in 1862. The states of California and Oregon, plus surrounding territories that were to become future states, were isolated from the eastern part of the country. The only way to reach the West was by sea or wagontrain; both were expensive, dangerous, and would take months to complete the journey. Also, during the Civil War, a direct rail line would help keep the west coast in the Union. The Central Pacific rail line was built east from Sacramento, California, and the Union Pacific rail line was built west from Omaha, Nebraska. It took until May 10, 1869, for the two railroads to join at Promontory Summit, Utah, and have connecting lines from coast to coast.

In the 1890s, Union Pacific extended its reach from Granger, Wyoming, to Portland, Oregon, after acquiring the Oregon Short Line. A line from Ogden, Utah, to Butte, Montana, was acquired at the same time. UP reached California in 1907 with a line from Ogden extending southwest to Los Angeles. A line to Kansas City from Denver would be acquired, and with branch lines and other secondary main lines, UP would operate 9700 miles of track.

In the 1980s, the railroad again began to grow. Western Pacific (1431 miles) was acquired on December 22, 1981. This gave UP a northern route to California from the Ogden-Salt Lake City area west across northern Nevada, through the Feather River Canyon, and on to Oakland. On December 22, 1982, Missouri Pacific (11,200 miles), and Missouri, Kansas & Texas (2200 miles) were acquired on August 12, 1988, giving UP access to Texas. On June 23, 1995, the Chicago & North Western (4,990 miles) was acquired and direct access to Chicago was achieved. The largest gain was on August 11, 1996, with the takeover of the combined Southern Pacific, Rio Grande (13,700 miles), which gave UP a southwest route from New Orleans to Los Angeles and up the coast to Portland, Oregon. The Donner Pass route to Salt Lake City and east to Denver put the total mileage of the railroad to 36,500 miles. Today, the Union Pacific faces the same challenges as BNSF in operating and maintaining such a large company. But for a railroad that's been in existence since 1862, is there any doubt that "The Overland Route" won't succeed?

Union Pacific's SD40-2 6934 and 3960 bring an eastbound train through the farm country in south central Nebraska, 10 miles west of Grand Island, on September 8,1997. 6934 was built for the Chicago & North Western in 1976, and 3960 was built for the Missouri Pacific in 1980.

On October 20, 1984, Union Pacific ran a 300-mile, round-trip excursion between Denver, Colorado and Laramie, Wyoming. DDA40X 6922 ran between Denver and Speer, Wyoming, where 4-6-6-4 3985 hauled the train west to Laramie over the new (1953) line. On return, 3985 took the train up the original line back to Speer, where 6922 powered the train back to Denver. Most heavier westbound trains out of Cheyenne use the new line with its easier grades. Although the line is nine miles longer, the westbound grade is .82% compared to 1.55% on the older line.

3985 is shown both at Laramie and on a photo runby heading toward Laramie. 3985 was built by ALCO in 1943 along with 24 more 4-6-6-4's for Union Pacific. UP had a total of 105 Challengers delivered between 1936 and 1944. Originally a coal burner, it has since been converted to oil. 3985 weighs 535 tons and is 122' in length. 69" drive wheels produce 97,350 lbs. tractive effort. The engine was pulled from display in Cheyenne and restored in 1981.

Union Pacific's other steam engine, 4-8-4 844, delivered in 1944 as UP's last new steam engine, has the distinction of being the only steam engine from a major railroad never to have been retired, being on UP's roster since 1944. Built as a passenger engine by ALCO, the 844 weighs 454 tons. UP had 44 of the class built between 1937 and 1944, with 80`` drive wheels which produce 63,800 lbs tractive effort.

DDA40X 6922 is on a photo runby on the northbound part of the Denver-to-Laramie excursion trip, on October 20, 1984. As 3985 heads east out of Laramie towards Sherman Hill, the train meets a westbound freight powered by DDA40X 6927 and two Norfolk Southern GE's. In the early 1980s UP removed the Centennials (the nickname for the DDA40X's because of the first ones being delivered to UP at the time of the 100th anniversary of the driving of the last spike at Promontory, Utah, on May 10, 1869) from service. With the traffic increased in 1984, about half of the 47 engines were put back in service and could be seen in system-wide use.

Union Pacific was the only buyer of the largest diesel electric locomotive ever built. Equipped with two V-16 645's under the long hood, the engine was rated at 6,600 hp. Other statistics were 98′ 5″ in length, 17′ 3″ from rail head to air horns, an 8,200-gallon fuel tank, operating weight of 275 tons, starting tractive effort of 136,000 lbs, and gearing for 90 mph. By early 1985, they were removed from service for the last time.

Only on the Union Pacific could the world's largest operating diesel electric and steam locomotives meet, as 6927, after just descending Sherman Hill, passes 3985 at 50mph. Once the freight had passed, the excursion train would be lined up for the mainline, and after a few more delays, would get a green light a little before dusk. A snow-storm encountered earlier in the day on the west-bound trip would still be present as the train reached the summit in the dark. The big Challenger would have no trouble with the sixteen-car train on the .82% eastbound grade of the original double-track line. Standing at the open window inside the vestibule of a passenger car for the climb, the combination of wind, snow, and coal smoke would add to the view of what mainline railroading across North America was like in the 1940s. About all one can do is say, "thanks, Uncle Pete," then stand back and enjoy the show.

Union Pacific has DDA40X 6936 at Cheyenne with its two operational steam engines, and occasionally gets out on the road on the passenger excursions; and if UP gets short handed, it goes back in freight service. Several have found their way to rail museums.

In 1966 Union Pacific took delivery of 83 SD40s. Pleased with the results, more SD40s and SD40-2's were purchased; by the early 1980s, over 800 were in service on the railroad. To the west of La Grande, Oregon, two of the numerous SD40-2's have just cut off from an eastbound train, on May 3, 1982. Most trains require helpers on these grades in the Blue Mountains or, in more recent times, distributed power. The photo was taken from the back of Amtrak's westbound Pioneer. The Chicago-to-Seattle train was one of the casualties of Amtrak's cutbacks in early May of 1997.

These two photos were taken at Portola, California, on Union Pacific's ex-Western Pacific, Salt Lake City, Utah-to-Oakland, California, mainline, on July 1, 1994. The top photo shows a Union Pacific excursion train that has just come in from Oakland. The E9 A-B-A's will power two round-trip excursions to Keddie Wye Bridge (to the west) per day, on July 2 and 3. The E9's were restored in the spring, giving UP more flexibility when running its excursions without the more costly expense of running their steam engines for extended periods. Below, a westbound loaded grain train departs the yard. The building in the left at back is the old Western Pacific diesel maintenance facility, now the home of the Portola Railroad Museum, which has 38 diesels from most of the major builders from the mid-1940s forward. They also have locomotive rentals, where you can choose between five different models to operate on their loop track.

Union Pacific E9A 951, E9B 963 and E9A 949 were built in 1955. Originally equipped with two V-12 567's per unit, which produced 2400 hp., the E9's were rebuilt with one 645 V-16, 2000 hp. engine. New GP control stands in the A-units and an upgraded braking system make for easier repairs if the units break down on the road. Union Pacific at one time had 40 E8's and 69 E9's to power their long-distance passenger trains. 951 is the only one Union Pacific kept with 963 and 949 going to Amtrak in the early 1970s. The two units were bought back by Union Pacific and by 1994 had the three units together with the excursion train to have a perfect reproduction of a classic 1950s passenger train. 951 is eastbound for Portola at Williams Loop on July 3, 1994.

To the left, the train is turning on Keddie Wye Bridge for the return trip to Portola, on July 2, 1994. The line in front of the E9's heads north 112 miles to Bieber, California, where it connects with the old Great Northern line through Bend, Oregon, and on to Burlington Northern's ex-Spokane, Portland and Seattle Railway in Washington State. On July 3, 1994, the train is at Reno Junction on the California-Nevada border. The train couldn't be turned at Portola, so had to run east 25 miles to Reno Junction where a branch leaves the mainline and runs to Reno, Nevada. Once turned, the train returned to Portola.

On April 28, 1995, the E9's are westbound at Reno Junction about to enter the 6000' Chilcoot Tunnel, which opened in 1909. East of the tunnel is barren and scrub brush, while to the west the Feather River provides rich farmlands of the Sierra Valley. On this day, the train would travel through the Feather River Canyon to Oroville. The next day, the plan was to run east to Keddie Wye Bridge and take the line north to Bieber.

Heavy rains that night closed the Bieber line, so the train continued east from Keddie Wye to Portola, then returned to Oroville. The train is shown at Blairsden, as the weather slowly deteriorated on April 28, 1995. Blairsden is located 11 miles west of Portola. Below, the train is crossing the Keddie Wye Bridge 35 miles west of Blairsden. Western Pacific built north of Keddie to meet the Great Northern in 1931.

Great Northern gained entrance into California and Western Pacific to the Pacific Northwest. The Keddie Wye Bridge was the spot where the last spike on the Western Pacific was driven in, on Nov 1, 1909. At its peak, Western Pacific had 1,227 mainline and 215 branch line miles of track. Although many people opposed the takeover of the Western Pacific In 1982, Union Pacific has spent millions of dollars upgrading the line, money that Western Pacific did not have. Train traffic on the line has increased significantly as a result.

These two photos show the same westbound train, on April 28, 1995. 15 miles west of Keddie Wye Bridge, the train snakes around an s-curve along the bank of the North Fork Feather River. From here down through the Feather River Canyon, rock and mudslides are commonplace. In the rainy season, all trains are escorted through the canyon by a hy-rail vehicle, which runs about one mile ahead of the train. Even with these precautions, the excursion train, on return to Oroville from Portola the following day, was delayed by two small slides.

The photo to the left shows the train 32 miles east of Oroville crossing the Feather River under the Route 70 highway bridge a few hundred feet above. Between Keddie and Oroville, the line runs 80 miles, most of the way through this rough canyon. From Oroville, the line runs 110 miles to Stockton and another 92 miles to Oakland.

Union Pacific inherited a large group of newer 6-axle GE's with the takeover of Chicago and North Western (C&NW) Railroad in 1995. 123 DASH9-44CW's and 33 AC4400CW's were added to Union Pacific's roster. C&NW had trouble with GE's in the 1970s, but gave them another try in 1989 with an order for 27 DASH8-40C's. They stayed with GE to the end, with 44 more DASH8's along with the 156 DASH 9's and AC4400s. Here, two DASH9-44CW's and a Union Pacific GE are eastbound coming into Blairsden, on September 26, 1996 with containers and trailers.

SD60M 6128 rolls a westbound train downhill in the upper part of Williams Loop, on September 26, 1996. Located about 15 miles west of Blairsden, the loop was opened in October of 1909. Almost a mile in circumference, when the track crosses under itself, it has dropped in elevation 45 feet on a 1% grade. One advantage of the old Western Pacific route is that from sea level in Oakland through the Sierra Nevada Mountains to Chilcoot Tunnel, at a little over 5000' in elevation, the line has a ruling grade of only 1%.

Williams Loop is less popular with rail photographers than the Tehachapi Loop to the south. With less traffic, and surrounded by trees, most of the loop is hidden. On September 26, 1996, an eastbound train enters the bottom part of the loop powered by SD40-2 3239, a SD40, C30-7, ex-SP SD45, and an ex-SP tunnel motor. The train slowly climbs uphill and crosses over itself. Unlike the Donner Pass line to the south, the old "Feather River Route" requires no helper districts to move the trains over the Sierra Nevadas. The 118 miles between Oroville and Portola was Western Pacific's Third Subdivision; now it is Union Pacific's Canyon Subdivision.

On September 24, 1996, 3800 hp., SD60M 6226 pulls an eastbound train five miles east of Portola. The train runs 25 miles from Portola through the Sierra Valley to Chilcoot Tunnel. The valley is surrounded by mountains, with the railroad running along the Feather River at the west end of the valley to reach Portola.

These two photos show two eastbound Union Pacific trains about to enter the 6000′ Chilcoot Tunnel, on September 26, 1996. In the tunnel, the summit of Beckwourth Pass is reached at a little over 5000′ and a 55-mile downgrade to Sand Pass begins. The route across Nevada and Utah is 580 miles in length.

The line has six summits it must cross in Nevada and through the Salt Lake Desert, then runs along the southern end of Great Salt Lake, arriving in ex-Rio Grande's Roper Yard in Salt Lake City. At one point the line drops to under 4000′, then climbs to 6000′ on two separate summits before dropping down to Salt Lake City at 4300′.

Western Pacific and Southern Pacific had a unique arrangement, started by the United States Railroad Administration in 1918, to make the 185 miles of parallel track of the two railroads between Winnemucca and Alazon, Nevada, more productive. All eastbounds from both roads would use Western Pacific, and all westbounds from both roads would use Southern Pacific. This kept trains moving, not having to wait for meets on the single-track lines. This worked out so well that it continues today on Union Pacific.

Two SD9043MAC's power a westbound train up Union Pacific's ex-Southern Pacific Donner Pass line, twenty miles west of Reno, Nevada, on September 27, 1997. When GM and GE announced their new 6000 hp. SD90MAC's and AC6000s in the mid-1990s, neither builder had an engine in production that would produce 6000 hp. GM installed 4300 hp. 16-710G3-ES engines, and GE installed 4400 hp 7FDL16's. Plans were to repower the engines later with the larger 6000 hp. engines when the problems were worked out. At this time, Union Pacific did have a few 6000 hp. engines from GM and GE in service. Bringing up the rear is ex-Southern Pacific SD45 8663 and two UP SD40-2's.

This was part of the first transcontinental railroad. The Central Pacific started building east from Sacramento in January of 1863, and it would take until 1868 before they crossed over the Sierra Nevada Mountains into Nevada. With its 7017-foot summit at Norden, and snowfall at up to forty feet deep a year, this line still can be a challenge to operate. Two rotary snowplows are stationed at Truckee, Ca. to keep the line open. From Roseville, just east of Sacramento, eastbounds climb from 200 feet to 7017 feet at Norden in 88 miles, with maximum grades of 2.2%. Westbounds from Sparks, Nevada, face a climb of 50 miles to the summit with maximum grades of 1.9%.

At the same location and a year earlier, F40PH 334 heads the westbound California Zephyr, on September 26, 1996. This train runs 2416 miles from Chicago, Illinois; through Omaha, Nebraska; Denver, Colorado; Salt Lake City, Utah; Reno, Nevada; to Oakland, California. San Francisco is reached from Oakland by Amtrak bus service.

The next three photos were taken 15 to 20 miles west of Laramie, on Union Pacific's mainline across southern Wyoming, on September 24, 1998. SD60M 6169 leads an eastbound double-stack train across the high plains. The elevations between Laramie west to Rock Springs range from 7,100' to 6,300'. With little protection from high winds and snow, this line across Wyoming is one of Union Pacific's toughest operating districts.

The last engine on the train is ex-Rio Grande SD40T-2 5346. Southern Pacific and Rio Grande were the only two railroads to order this model from EMD. Both railroads operated through many tunnels along their lines and were experiencing problems with trailing engines overheating and shutting down in the tunnels. Instead of having the fans on the top of the locomotive and pulling air through the radiators, the fans were mounted below to push pressurized air through the radiators, giving them increased cooling over conventional locomotives. The low air intake opening along the walkway gave these GM locomotives a distinctive look, and they received the nickname "Tunnel Motors."

DASH8-41CW's 9498 and 9481 have trailers and containers heading east, on September 24, 1998. On this morning, westbound traffic was light, but six eastbounds were running about 10 minutes behind each other. In the late 1990s, Union Pacific was running around 80 trains a day across their Wyoming Division, which begins at Cheyenne and runs west to Ogden, Utah.

GE DASH8-40C 9180 and an ex-SP B39-8 haul an eastbound auto rack train, on September 24, 1998. To the right of the train, exhaust smoke can be seen of another eastbound following this train, which in turn is 10 minutes behind another eastbound. In 15 miles this train will be at Laramie.

SD60M 6339 is westbound ten miles west of Laramie, on May 6, 1995, with a mixed freight train. Track work or a slower train must be ahead, since 6339 is running on the eastbound main. The land across southern Wyoming is barren and sparsely populated, generating little on-line traffic for the railroad. As in the past, the line serves mostly as a conveyor belt to move traffic between the East and West.

SD50 5094 and SD40-2 3137 rest in the Laramie yard, on September 24, 1998. Laramie has a welded-rail plant where jointed rails are welded into quarter-mile lengths. Later that day I, caught 5094 and 3137 on Sherman Hill heading east, with a welded-rail train for the Nebraska triple-track project.

Track crews reached Cheyenne, Wyoming, in November of 1867. In the spring of 1868 building would resume, and by the end of the year the Wyoming-Utah border would be reached 425 miles to the west. From Cheyenne to Laramie, 50 miles to the west, Union Pacific would build up and over Sherman Hill. At Cheyenne, 6060′ elevation, trains climb to the summit (8013′) and then run downhill into Laramie (7165′). Despite its relatively easy climb (1.55%), Sherman Hill remains one of the better-known rail landmarks of the West. A westbound double-stack train is ten miles west of Cheyenne climbing Sherman Hill, powered by an ex-Chicago and North Western GE and an ex-Rio Grande tunnel motor, on September 25, 1998.

A C&NW GE leads another stack train eastbound at the same location, on May 8, 1995. Heavy clouds and fog were moving in, and by the next morning the late spring storm would leave, on Laramie and to the west, two feet of snow.

SD60M 6340 is on a mixed train dropping downhill at Borie, on September 11, 1997, on another storm-threatening day. Amtrk's Pioneer would turn south here and continue on to Denver. Since Cheyenne wasn't reached by the train, a shuttle bus was used to transfer passengers from the city to meet the train at this remote spot.

Most heavier westbound trains use the easier, 1953, .82% line over Sherman. Most eastbounds and lighter trailer and container trains westbound use the original mainline. Westbounds out of Cheyenne on the old line have a climb of 1.55 %, which starts on the western edge of Cheyenne as the mainline passes under BNSF's ex-Colorado and Southern Railroad bridge. Eastbounds from Laramie only have a .82% climb. This line was famous in the 1950s, with Union Pacific running its biggest power until July of 1959, during summer and fall traffic surges, mostly over Sherman Hill between Cheyenne and Laramie, the 132', 600-ton, 4-8-8-4 Big Boys. Above, on May 6, 1995, SD60M 6147 has a double-stack westbound about 20 miles west of Cheyenne.

At the same location with another westbound double-stack, on September 11, 1997, three six-axle GE's pass under the competition: New York City to Oakland, California, Interstate 80.

A year later, on September 25, 1998, two ex-Chicago and North Western GE's bring an eastbound trailer train downhill in the late afternoon. It seemed like the route of the "400" engines were everywhere, but slowly they would fade away as Union Pacific repainted them yellow and gray when the engines were cycled through their shops for major overhauls.

SD50 5094 drops downhill with a welded-rail train twenty miles west of Cheyenne, on September 24,1998, heading for Union Pacific's triple-track project in Nebraska. Once the jointed rails were welded, they were placed on flat cars designed with rollers; 40 rails 5 stacks high and 8 rails per row made up the train.

The rails bend with the train as the head end curves to the right and under Interstate 80. When the rails arrived on the job site, they were rolled off the flat cars, unaffected by all the twists and turns they encountered from Laramie.

Diesels wait at the fueling and sanding racks in Cheyenne, on May 5, 1995. To the left is what remains of the one-time 48-stall roundhouse. Today, the 7-stall building houses Union Pacific's historic steam and diesel collection. To the right stands the Cheyenne train station, built in 1887, where east- and westbound trains stop to re-crew.

Two SD9043MAC's pull an eastbound coal train on the North Platte Subdivision, 10 miles east of Northport, Nebraska, on September 27, 1998. One wonders why Union Pacific decided on such a small Union Pacific shield on the nose of its new GM's and GE's.

The next five photos were taken on Archer Hill, east of Cheyenne. East bounds have a .70% grade to the summit 10 miles east of Cheyenne. On September 26, 1998, AC44/60CW 7031 headed eastbound. Equipped with a 4400 hp., V-16, the engine may someday have the 6000 hp. 7HDL16A, 250 mm bore, 320 mm stroke, four-cycle engine installed. That figures out to 961 cubic inches per cylinder, for a total of 15,376-cubic-inch displacement. Cheyenne can be seen in the left of the photo.

DASH9-44CW 9734 was westbound as it descended Archer Hill, on September 26, 1998. The top of the hill can be seen in the background. With a crew change in Cheyenne, the train faced the climb up Sherman Hill and on to the west coast.

SD60 6044 and ex-Southern Pacific SD40T-2 8548 had a trailer train eastbound. With the mergers and buying of new power, Union Pacific added around 1000 new, six-axle, General Electric locomotives to its roster from the early 1990s through 2000. General Motors locomotives received during the same period totaled around 660 units.

SD90 43MAC 8203 headed east with a mixed train. 8203 may someday receive the 6000 hp. GM16V265H replacement engine. This V-16 engine has a four-cycle, 265 mm bore, 300mm stroke, which figures out to 1010 cubic inches per cylinder, for a total of 16,160 cubic-inch displacement.

This last photo of an eastbound train on Archer Hill shows that not all perishable traffic has been lost to trucks; about 50 refrigerated boxcars of West Coast produce make up the head end of the train. It is powered by two 4000 hp., GE DASH 8-40C's, the last type of engine Union Pacific received with regular cabs. Since that time, the engines have new, wide or safety cabs that give crews more protection in the event of a collision.

SD9043MAC 8266 heads a westbound train ten miles west of Sidney, Nebraska, on September 26, 1998. By the end of the 1990s, Uncle Pete had 309 SD9043MAC's and 62 SD90MAC's. In April 2000, UP began to receive the first of 1000, 4000 hp. SD70M's, the largest single order ever placed for a single model. These engines have D.C. traction and the older 26L air brakes. Union Pacific's decision was based on the AC locomotives having a higher out-of-service rate because of the new electronically controlled air brakes, AC traction, and computer problems. Shop crews throughout UP's system are more familiar with the older, tried and true systems of the SD70M's.

8266 is seen a few miles farther west. The trailing GP38-2 is dwarfed by the 80 foot 2 inch, 212 ton SD9043MAC. 8266's 5,800 fuel tank rides higher off the rail than the trailing units, which give it more protection from debris along the track. The distinguishing difference between the 43MAC's and the 90MAC's is that the 6000 hp. units have 45° angles along the hood ahead of the radiators. As impressive as 8266 is, the locomotive has 2300 less horsepower, is over 18 feet shorter, and has two fewer axles than UP's DDA40X's built by GM between 1969 and1971. Known for their high-speed running and large appetite for fuel, the eight-axle "Big Jacks" had the reputation of being able to pass anything on the road but a fueling rack.

In 1998, Union Pacific had a handful of the SD90MAC's running on their lines. Here, 8510 leads an eastbound coal train at O'Fallon's, Nebraska, on September 30, 1998. This is where UP's North Platte Subdivision joins the mainline. Between North Platte and east to Gibbon, a third mainline was added to handle the ever-increasing traffic. The 6000 hp. engines have a 200,000 lb. starting and170,000 lb. continuous tractive effort. In comparison, UP's 25 Big Boys had 135,375 maximum tractive effort. The highest horsepower level for a Big Boy ever recorded was when 4016 achieved 6,290 hp. on a test run April 3, 1943.

Two more ex-C & NW GE's are on a westbound stack train, one mile east of the Wyoming-Nebraska border, on September 26, 1998. Behind the lead engine's nose are snow fences Union Pacific has built to keep snow drifts from covering the line. As with Wyoming, the line across Nebraska has little protection against the winters.

SD40-2 3148 had an eastbound trailer train 20 miles east of North Platte, Nebraska, on September 8, 1997. The trailing, ex-Southern Pacific SD45 looks like it hasn't been painted since being received new from GM. This unit won't be around long enough, with all the GM and GE orders placed by UP, to be repainted.

Eight miles east of North Platte, two eastbounds paced each other with the covered hopper train slowly overtaking the coal train. DASH9-44CW 9706 and ex-Missouri Pacific SD40-2 4268 had a 70-mph run east, while AC4400 CW 6685 and DASH8-40C 9104 on the heavier coal train had a 60 mph. speed limit. UP's Nebraska Division extends from Council Bluffs, Iowa, and runs west to Cheyenne.

SD9043MAC 8268 brings an empty coal train west into North Platte, on September 30, 1998. Union Pacific spent four years and 327 million dollars on the 108 miles between North Platte and Gibbon, to turn it into a triple-track, 70 mph., and 150-trains-a-day mainline. With container and trailer traffic growing and more coal coming out of the Power River region, the old, double-track line was beyond its capacity. The line is the world's busiest rail freight corridor, handling in excess of 300 million tons per year.

A few miles west of Grand Island, on September 8, 1997, AC4400 CW 6619 and a SD9043MAC were found with another load of eastbound coal. At Gibbon, a mainline branches off and heads southeast through Hastings, Kansas City, and St Louis. Lines then head south though Oklahoma and Texas. A lot of traffic leaves the mainline for these routes, so east of Gibbon the line reverts to a double track.

Off home rails, UP SD70M 4423 and SD40-2 3395 worked an eastbound CSX train under the ex-Western Maryland's Salisbury Viaduct west of Meyersdale, Pa., on September 16, 2004. UP would add to their initial order of 1000 SD70M's, bringing the total to 1400 by the end of 2004. A UP tradition would return, with the new locomotives being delivered with wings.

The Chicago & North Western gained entry to the Orin Subdivision with help from Union Pacific and the Interstate Commerce Commission, by 1984. 76 million was paid for a 50 percent interest from Shawnee Junction, 10 miles north of Bridger Junction and north 91 miles to Coal Creek. Later, 11 more miles north to East Caballo Junction was obtained for 27 million dollars. From UP's North Platte Subdivision at Joyce, Nebraska, 56 miles of new railroad would be built north to Crandall, Wyoming, then west 45 miles to Shawnee, C.& NW's old "Cowboy Line" would be rebuilt. From here, a six-mile connection would be built to Shawnee Junction. With the takeover of C&NW, Union Pacific has half ownership of the Orin Subdivision. The top photo shows three UP GE's moving south out of Bill, Wy., with a coal train, on September 18, 1998.

Five miles south of Bill, on the same day, another coal train headed south.

The bottom photo shows AC4400CW 6785 shoving a loaded coal train 15 miles west of Northport, Nebraska, on September 29, 1998. UP used Distributed Power on many of its coal trains, with the engineer controlling the helpers by radio control. With a helper in back keeping the slack bunched up, a coupler break is less likely on this 15,000-ton train.

A ex-Chicago & North Western, six-axle GE brings a double-stack train eastbound, ten miles west of Sidney, Nebraska, on September 29, 1998.

Union Pacific's E9's are eastbound with a Keddie Wye Bridge to Portola, Ca. excursion train at Williams Loop, on July 2, 1994.

Donated by the Union Pacific, DDA40X 6946 rests at the Portola Railroad Museum, on September 8, 1993. 6946 was the last of 47 ordered by the UP, being built in September of 1971. Those four-axle trucks look like they would straighten out every curve they passed through.

Ex-Chicago & North Western DASH9-44CW 8646 and an ex-Southern Pacific Tunnel Motor bring an eastbound trailer and container train up Archer Hill, east of Cheyenne, on September 26, 1998.

Ex-Southern Pacific Tunnel Motor SD45T-2 9260, built in 1972, is on a westbound Union Pacific train descending Archer Hill, on September 26, 1998. Like the SD40T-2, the 70' 8"-long SD45T-2 was designed with the air intakes just above the frame to pull in cooler and cleaner air when operating through tunnels. SP would be the only railroad to order the 3,600 hp., SD45T-2, and 249 were built by GM between 1972 and 1975. SP also had 239 of the smaller, 3000 hp., SD40T-2's, and Rio Grande had 73 of them, having been built between 1974 and 1980. Between 1966 and 1970, SP would also acquire 355 standard SD45's as well as ten SDP45's for passenger service. SP's distinct roof-mounted bell stands out on the 9260, against the bank in the background.

A westbound Union Pacific train snakes its way through the Feather River Canyon as it drops downhill passing under the Route 70 highway bridge at Pulga on July 4, 1994.

Chapter 5
Cass Scenic Railroad

The Cass Scenic Railroad has been hauling tourists from Cass, West Virginia, since June 15, 1963. The town was created in 1900 when Joseph Cass, president of the West Virginia Pulp and Paper Company, built a saw mill at this location. At one time the town had 2000 residents, but by 1960 the timber was cut and the mill was closed. The railroad line was saved and is now operated by the West Virginia State Park System.

The first photo shows ex-Western Maryland Shay 6 outside the shops at Cass, on September11, 2004, and the second photo is a side view of its' three cylinders and front drive shaft, as they appeared on May 1, 1993.
This locomotive was the last Shay built by the Lima Locomotive Works in Lima, Ohio. Built for the Western Maryland line in 1945, "Big Six" was used on the 9.1% grades of the Chaffee Coal Branch, which connected with the Cumberland, Md.-to-Elkins, West Virginia, Thomas Subdivision, 41 miles west of Cumberland. "Big Six" went to the B&O Railroad Museum in 1953 and was leased to Cass by the Chessie System in 1980. At 162 tons, the locomotive is 66 feet long with 48-inch wheels, giving it an overall height of 15' 2". Tractive effort for this ultimate Shay is 59,740 lbs. Of all the geared locomotives, Shays were the most popular with lumber companies; 2770 were built between 1880 and 1945. The locomotive has a unique look, with the three cylinders mounted vertically ahead of the cab, which connects to a drive shaft that powers each truck through beveled gears. The boiler is off-set to the left, to compensate for all the weight on the right side. These locomotives could be ordered with two or three cylinders; two, three, or four trucks; and weighted between 10 and 162 tons.

Outside the shops at Cass, on September 7, 2003, are Shay's 2 and 11. The 2 was built in 1928 and worked for lumbering operations on the West Coast. The 90-ton engine came to Cass in 1970, having been converted from oil to coal burning in 1982. The 11 was built in 1923 for the Hutchinson Lumber Company, in Butte County, California. Cass acquired the 100-ton engine in 1998 from the San Diego Railroad Museum. It was converted from burning oil to coal in 2000.

Western Maryland's engine 6 is on a siding half-way up the line at Whittaker, as Shay 2 and Heisler 6 pass by. Their offset boilers can clearly be seen in this photo, taken on May 1, 1993.

Engines 2 and 6 take water at Cass, on May 2, 1993, for the trip to Bald Knob. Behind me is where the sawmill once stood, but in 1982 it was destroyed by arson. Before the fire, there were plans to save the mill. The company store remains, and is the main focal point of the town, with all trains departing from it. Company houses also have been restored and can be rented.

Heisler 6 was built in 1929, for Bostonia Coal, Clay & Meadow River Lumber Company, of New Bethlehem, Pa. It weights 100 tons. The Heisler Locomotive Works was located in Erie, Pa., and between 1891 and 1940 they built more than 600 engines. These locomotives were designed with two cylinders in V-formation, connecting to a driveshaft running in the center of the locomotive between the trucks. Only one axle on each truck was attached to the drive shaft by beveled gears, much like a truck differential, with the other axle getting it's power from the side rod attached to the power axle.

Engines 2 and 6 are in the yard at Cass, on May 1, 1993. An advantage the geared engines had over the standard rod type engine was that all of their weight was used for traction. With a regular steam engine, the water and coal being hauled behind in the tender was necessary to produce steam, but was extra weight the engine couldn't make use of. Most geared engines had a top speed of 20 mph, but since most operated on steep and rough track, this speed was rarely achieved.

To get to the 4842' elevation of Bald Knob, the railroad has two switchbacks and grades as steep as 11% in the 12 miles of track. Above Whittaker, a branch was rebuilt in the early 1990s that runs downhill to Spruce, and connects with the ex-Western Maryland line that runs north to Elkins, W.Va. Heisler 6 was across from the shops, on April 30, 1993, being prepared for another trip up the mountain. The three-truck engine was one of the largest built at Erie, Pa. The top of the water tank, seen in the left of the photo, served the logging engines at Cass, along with engines of the Chesapeake & Ohio on their Greenbrier Division.

This engine represents the third major geared locomotive builder, Climax Manufacturing Company, of Corry, Pa. Between 1888 and 1928, around 1035 were constructed. The Climax, like the Heisler, could be ordered with two or three trucks, the largest weighing 100 tons. The cylinders ran along the boiler at an angle of 22.5 degrees and had a driveshaft in the center, like the Heisler, but each axle was powered by the drive shaft with beveled gears, eliminating the need for side rods. This 70-ton, three-truck Climax was built in 1919, for Moore- Keppel & Company of Ellamore, W. Va., to haul logs and coal on its Middle Fork Railroad. Cass acquired the locomotive from Robert Johnson, in 1971, but was caught in the shop fire in 1972. Here, it is shown outside the shop, on April 30, 1993. In September of 2001, restoration on the locomotive was started, and it is expected to take up to seven years to bring #6 back to operating condition.
The Durbin & Greenbrier Valley Railroad operates from Durbin, W. Va., 18 miles north of Cass. They run south of town five miles on the old Chesapeake and Ohio Railway's Greenbrier Division. This line was completed in 1902. It ran from Whitcomb on C&O's Newport News, Va. to Chicago mainline, north through Cass, and on to Durbin, at milepost 95.55.

The line extended north five miles from Durbin to serve saw mills and the Pocahontas Tanning Company. The Coal and Iron Railway was built south from Elkins and reached Durbin by 1903. Freight service ended on the line on December 28, 1978. The rails between Cass and Durbin remain, but there are washouts. Climax #3 was parked by the station, on September 8, 2002. The two-truck, 55-ton engine was built in 1910, for Moore-Keppel & Company. The Connecticut Electric Railway Association bought #3 in 1960 and restored it in 1990. The locomotive was put up for sale and the highest bid went to the D & G.V. Engine #3 arrived back in West Virginia in the spring of 2002.

Chapter 6
Rio Grande Narrow Gauge

Denver & Rio Grande Western's three-foot, narrow gauge lines at one time had a total of 805 miles of track. Construction started at Denver, in July 1871, and headed south to Pueblo, with a line running west to Salt Lake City, Utah. From Pueblo south, the line ran to Antonito, Colorado, with one branch running to Santa Fe, New Mexico, and another line running west from Antonito through Chama, New Mexico, and on to Durango, Colorado. From here, a line headed north 45 miles to Silverton, and a different line ran south to Farmington, New Mexico. By the early 1880s, the lines were complete. Before long, the Rio Grande Railroad standard gauged all the lines north of Antonito, with the track between here and Alamosa, 30 miles north, being dual gauge to handle narrow and standard-gauge cars. As hard as it is to believe, Rio Grande continued to run steam-powered, narrow-gauge, freight trains until the late summer of 1968.

Two segments of the line were saved: the 45 miles between Durango and Silverton and the 64 miles over Cumbres Pass, between Chama and Antonito. The line between Chama and Antonito is now called the Cumbres and Toltec Scenic Railroad. The line was completed to Chama on January 18, 1881. From Chama, at 7863′ elevation, the line climbs toward Cumbres Pass at 10,015′, 13 miles north, on grades as steep as 4%. K-36 2-8-2's engines 488 and 489 have reached the 10,015′ summit, with an Antonito-bound train, on October 10, 1990. The 488 will cut off and return to Chama, while 489 takes the train to Antonito at 7888′. From here, it's mostly downhill on a ruling 1.5% grade for 51 miles. 489 is shown 8 miles later, as it had just passed through the horseshoe curve at the Los Pinos water tank. Snow was beginning to appear in the Colorado high country.

Thanks to a group of British rail fans who chartered freight trains for a couple of days, I had the opportunity to see freight operations along the line. These three photos show the 463 coming through the Chama Yards with a short tank car train, on October 7, 1997. The 463 is the oldest and smallest locomotive on the Cumbres and Toltec line, having been built by Baldwin in 1903. Rio Grande had fifteen of the 2-8-2 class K-27 engines, with an operating weight of 112 tons and 40″ drive wheels, producing 27,000 lbs. tractive effort. As the train passed by, these photos could easily be mistaken for the early 1900s, if not for the radio held by the brakeman and the sports utility vehicles in the background.

In what by all rights should have become an abandoned right of way in the late 1960s, rails are still spiked 36″ apart, and four live 2-8-2's are in the yard. Shortly, a double-headed passenger train, followed by a double-headed freight train, departed for Cumbres Pass. Amazing.

The narrow-gauged lines survived for several reasons. Rio Grande's equipment on these lines was in reasonably good shape. There was enough traffic on the lines to keep them operational, but not enough to justify the expense to install standard-gauge lines. Traffic included lumber, livestock, crude oil, concentrates, coal, consumer goods, and oil and gas well casings, as well as pipe for the Farmington gas field. By the 1950s, highways along the narrow gauge line were improved, cutting into the line's freight and passenger business. The narrow gauge's longevity was the key to its survival. The last steam-powered, narrow-gauge line in North America drew a lot of attention from rail fans and historic groups, resulting in the saving of two segments of this famous line.

Engine 488 is at Cumbres Pass after helping the Antonito-bound passenger train, on October 10, 1990. Rio Grande had 10 of the Class K-36 2-8-2 types, numbered 480 to 489. These engines were built by Baldwin in 1925, with an operating weight of 144 tons and a tractive effort of 36,200 lbs. All of the Rio Grande narrow gauge 2-8-2's were built with the drive wheels inside the frame, with the counter-balances and side rods on the outside of the frame. 488 is also equipped with a heavy snowplow for not only snow, but large stones that might fall on the right-of-way. The class K-36's have an overall length of 68', height of 13'4", width of 10'5", and have 44" drive wheels.

Engine K-37 497 is on the head end with engine 463 pushing the back of an 18-car freight train climbing the 4% grade, three miles from the summit, on October 6, 1997. Rio Grande had ten of the 2-8-2 class K-37's, numbered 490 through 499. These were the largest of the narrow-gauge engines, with a 154-ton operating weight, producing 37,100 lbs. tractive effort with 44" drive wheels. The K-37 class was unique in that they at one time were standard gauge 2-8-0s, rebuilt by Rio Grande's Burnham Shops at Denver, between 1928 and 1930, to narrow-gauge locomotives.

This photo shows a double-headed train out of Chama behind engines 463 and 487, on October 8, 1997. This spot is called Cresco, and besides the water tank at one time it had a siding. The train still has a five-mile climb before reaching the summit.

Actual air miles between Chama and Antonito are 34, but the Rio Grande was forced to build 64 miles of railroad track to keep the grades tolerable. Between mileposts 283 and 330, the line crosses back and forth between Colorado and New Mexico eleven times. With the high elevations and snow, this line only operates from mid-May through mid-October. The two photos show 488 and 489 climbing to Cumbres Pass, with the Antonito-bound train, on October 10, 1990. The first photo shows the train about six miles out of Chama. The Wolf Creek trestle at Lobato has a weight restriction, so the engines must unhook and run across separately. The grade is noticeable, as the two engines are shown a few miles uphill from Lobato.

On October 6, 1997, after a meet with the 18-car freight train powered by 497 and 463 at Cumbres Pass Summit, 488 brings the Chama-bound passenger train downhill. Above 488's smoke stack, the grade can be seen cut-in along the top of the hillside. Out of sight to the right of the photo, the track circles around the hill and arrives at the 10,015' summit.

At the Chama Yard, engines 463 and 497 wait to take an eastbound, eighteen-car freight train up Cumbres Pass, on October 6, 1997. 463 would be purchased by Gene Autry in 1955, for his Melody Ranch in California. He would later donate it to the city of Antonito, were the locomotive would be returned to service on the Cumbres & Toltec Scenic Railroad. 497 started out in 1902 as a standard-gauge, C-41 2-8-0 1003 built by Baldwin. In 1930 the locomotive was rebuilt into narrow gauge K-37 2-8-2 497.

In what could be described as a working museum, the Chama Yard hasn't changed much since the 1930s. A double-spouted water tank can be seen at the east end of the yard, along with the large coal tipple, built in 1924. Unused since the Cumbres & Toltec started in 1971, the tipple will be restored in the near future to operating condition. There is also a shop for working on locomotives and rolling stock. The K-36 487 will be the helper engine to Cumbres Pass on the passenger train today.

The 487 steams at Chama, on October 7, 1997, and is equipped with one of the Rio Grande's large plows. Intended for snow, the plow would help with removing any trees and other debris from the right-of-way that 487 may encounter.

The 463 and 497 are about two miles out of Chama, with the eighteen-car, eastbound freight train, on October 6, 1997.

463 would be cut into the back of the train farther up the line, and is shown three miles from the summit, having just crossed Route 17. My 1997 F-250 pick-up truck and other vehicles date the photo; without them, this image could easily pass as being decades earlier.

The 4% grade is apparent as lead engine 497 has reached Windy Point, with the summit just around the bend. This line gives an unparalleled view of what narrow-gauge railroading was like in the early part of the 20th century, along the Denver & Rio Grande's "Scenic Line of the World."

Chapter 7
White Pass and Yukon Railroad

The White Pass and Yukon Railroad is a three-foot line that runs from Skagway, Alaska, 110 miles north to Whitehorse in the Yukon. Started in May of 1898 and completed in July of 1900, the line was built to haul people and supplies for the gold strikes in the Klondike north of Whitehorse. By the time the railroad was complete, the Gold Rush had passed, but the railroad would continue to operate for the next 82 years, linking the two cities. Cruise ships now dock where containers and ore concentrates use to be loaded onto ships. Until 1982, more than 500,000 tons of lead, zinc, and copper concentrates a year were hauled by the railroad to the Skagway docks. A decline in metal prices and an improved highway between Skagway and Whitehorse caused the railroad to close in 1982. In 1988, the line reopened as a tourist hauler, and by the late 1990s was hauling 258,000 people a year.

In 1991, trains ran from Skagway north 28 miles to Fraser, British Columbia. At Skagway, on September 11, 1991, three GE's have returned from Fraser. 2-8-2 73, built by Baldwin, is on the side track. Between 1954 and 1966, eleven of the GE90s were built by GE at Erie, Pa. Given road numbers 90 to 100, these engines are powered by an ALCO 251 six-cylinder engine and are rated at 890 to 990 hp.

From Skagway, at sea level, 21 miles of track with a ruling grade of 3.9% is needed to reach White Pass Summit, at 2865' elevation. On September 12, 1991, three GE's head uphill about 8 miles north of Skagway. On the return trip, the train is shown descending the grade about 17 miles from Skagway. Rails remain in place to Whitehorse, and maybe in the future the mines in the Yukon will reopen, with Skagway becoming again an export harbor for ore concentrates. Passenger trains started running 67 miles north to the town of Carcross in the summer of 2001.

On September 11, 1991, engine 73 rests beside two GE's, that are repainted to original colors, outside the Skagway station. The little 2-8-2, built in 1947, would be the last narrow-gauge, steam locomotive that Baldwin would build for a domestic railroad. 73 was taken out of service in 1964 and rebuilt, at Skagway, in 1979. Cruise ships, docked to the left, bring many people to ride the trains over White Pass Summit.

On September 12, 1991, a southbound passenger train drops downhill past the 215' high Dead Horse Gulch steel cantilever bridge that was completed in 1901 and is located two miles below White Pass Summit. It was replaced in 1969 with a smaller bridge and a 750 foot-tunnel a short distance up the canyon. Dead Horse Gulch received its name because of the thousands of pack animals that died and were left by prospectors along the trail, as they continued north to the gold fields. One can still hike the Trail of 1898 from Skagway over White Pass.

About 15 miles north of Skagway, the flat nose of GE90 #91 gave a clear view as the train headed for the summit, on September 14, 1991. The track averages a climb of 141 feet per mile, with the steepest being 206 feet per mile. As with the Rio Grande, narrow gauge was chosen for its lower construction cost. With the railroad having no connections with any other rail lines, there was never a need to consider standard gauge for the "Gateway to the Yukon."

Chapter 8
Here and There

The California State Railroad Museum at Sacramento, opened in 1981, has become one of the premier railroad museums in the United States, with 500,000 visitors a year. The museum is at an appropriate location, the site where the Central Pacific Railroad started in the early 1860s. The Sacramento Shops, located close by and owned by Union Pacific, is now part of the museum and will house equipment currently outside The Sacramento Shops were constructed in the late 1860s and built their first locomotive for Central Pacific in 1872. 200 steam engines were built here and thousands of steam and diesel engines were rebuilt at the shops over the years. By the late 1990s, Union Pacific had shifted operations 18 miles east to the ex-SP Roseville Yard.

The photo shows the new museum building, on September 15, 1993, with Southern Pacific E9 6051, Western Pacific F7 913, and (barely visible behind 913) the Santa Fe 2-6-2 1010.

Warbonnet F7A 347C and F3B 347B, both built for Santa Fe in 1949, are outside the museum, on September 15, 1993.

On May 23, 1983, Southern Pacific's SD9 4301 is at a siding with a transfer caboose at Sacramento. The photo was taken from Amtrak's southbound Coast Starlight. SP had 43 1500 hp, SD7's and 150 1750 hp. SD9's built between 1952 and 1956, which helped spell the end to SP's Cab Forwards and 4-8-4 Daylights. Well liked by the railroad, the 43 SD7's and 144 SD9's were rebuilt by the railroad in the 1970s, to Dash 2 standards. Wouldn't 4301 fit in well at the museum with its old number and "Black Widow" paint?

Milwaukee Road SDL39 584 and two SD40-2's are passed by the eastbound Empire Builder, on June 15, 1984, just east of St. Paul. Milwaukee Road was the only buyer of the SDL39, only 55' long and powered by a 12-cylinder 645E engine, which produced 2300 hp. The ten engines were designed for branch line work, with light rail and bridge limits, and at 20.8 tons per axle could run just about anywhere. The Milwaukee Road was the last major line to reach the Pacific Northwest in 1909, and at its height it operated 11,000 miles of track. Traffic on the western end had always been light. By 1974, both sections of their electric divisions—the 440 mile, Avery, Idaho, to Harlowton, Montana, section and the 207-mile section across the Saddle and Cascade Mountains—were diesel powered. Bankruptcy in 1977 caused the Milwaukee Road, by 1980, to abandon the line from Miles City, Montana, to the West Coast, and by 1986 "America's Resourceful Railroad" would disappear with the takeover by SOO Line.

Montana Rail Link SD45 371 and four older six-axle GM's haul an eastbound train uphill on 1.4 percent grade of Mullen Pass, 60 miles east of Missoula, Mt., on September 17, 1997. Westbound trains face a 2.2 percent grade. Northern Pacific built the line through this area in 1882-1883, and it was the first northern route to Seattle and Tacoma, with the last spike driven at Gold Creek, Montana, on September 7, 1883. With BNSF runs through, and MRL's own trains, 20 trains a day are not uncommon on this single-track line. Engine 371 was built for the Pennsylvania Railroad, in December of 1967, as their number 6178. Five railroads and nearly 30 years later, the 65' 9 ½", 182-ton engine can still provide "Hustle Muscle," (the logo was placed on both sides of the long hood of the first SD45 ordered by a railroad, #400 built in May 1966 for the Great Northern). As of 2005, the 371 was still in service, but with the railroad placing an order for 16 SD70ACe's, Montana Rail Links' fleet of 64 SD45's will start to be thinned out.

Canadian National Railway's SD40-2's 5298 and 5248 pull an east-bound train out of Prince George, B.C., on May19, 1983. Canada-ian Natuional (CN) was the first railroad to equip their locomotives with safety cabs. In 1922, CN was formed to operate five railroads that were in financial trouble and were under control of the government of Canada. The result was a 22,000-mile system from the ports of Prince Rupert and Vancouver in British Columbia to Halifax, Nova Scotia, on the east coast. In 1999, CN gained control of the 3450-mile Illinois Central, giving them access to Mexico, and in 2001 the Wisconsin Central was acquired, giving them direct access to Chicago.

On August 31, 1982, Delaware and Hudson Railroad GP39-2 7602 heads a southbound train north of Binghamton, New York, on the line to Schenectady and on to Montreal, Canada. The company dates to 1823, when the Delaware and Hudson Canal Company was chartered to build a canal to carry coal from Pennsylvania to New York City. D&H stayed out of Conrail in 1976, but gained trackage rights on Conrail to Buffalo, Newark, Philadelphia, and Washington.

In 1980, D&H bought the ex-Lackawanna mainline, from Binghamton, N.Y., to Scranton, Pa. and removed its line between the two cities over Ararat Summit. The ex-Delaware, Lackawanna and Western Railroad mainline had been rebuilt between 1912 and 1915, with less severe grades than the D&H line. Guilford Transportation Industries took control of the D&H in 1984, and by 1988 "The Bridge Line" was in bankruptcy. The Susquehanna Railroad then operated the line until December 31, 1991, when Canadian Pacific purchased the Delaware and Hudson plus trackage rights, for 25 million dollars.
Canadian Pacific SD40-2 5795 leads a northbound train out of Scranton, and is near the 2375' long, 240' high Tunkhannock Viaduct, at Nicholson, Pa., in September of 1994. Made of cement and opened to traffic on November 7, 1915, the bridge is located 19 miles west of Scranton.

The East Broad Top Railroad (EBT) began operation in 1873. Hauling mixed freight and coal, the three-foot gauge line eventually built over 32 miles of track. Coal was hauled east to the Pennsylvania Railroad, at Mt. Union, Pa. and transferred to standard-gauge cars. In 1956, the EBT was shut down, and Kovalchick Salvage Company bought the line. But instead of scrapping it, the entire line was left intact, including the station, roundhouse, and machine shops at Rockhill Furnace in Orbisonia. In 1960, five miles of track reopened east of Rockhill Furnace for excursion trains.
64-ton 2-8-2 #14, built by Baldwin in 1912, one of six Mikado's still on the EBT, is seen in front of Orbisonia station, on September 14, 2003, before the first of three trips that day. In the background are the shops and yards, giving a scene that hasn't change since the #14 arrived here 90-some years ago.

In 1901 the Pennsylvania Railroad began electrifying its lines in the New York City area. Between 1928 and 1938, Pennsy started the intercity electrification project that would bring 673 route miles on 2,158 miles of track under the 11,000 volt system. The New York City to Philadelphia route was electrified by January 1933, followed by the Philadelphia to Washington route in January 1935, and the final Philadelphia to Harrisburg segment in service by January 1938. Plans at one time were to electrify the line from Harrisburg to Pittsburgh, but that never materialized. Think how different our images of Pennsy's Middle Division and Horseshoe Curve would be with 8,000 hp. GGI's instead of Pennsy's 4-6-2 K4s, 2-10-0 I1'S, and 4-8-2 M1's.

These two photos were taken from Philadelphia's 30th Street Station, which opened on December 15, 1933. The top photo, taken on May 27, 1984, shows E60s, F40PH's GP7's, RS3's and AEM-7's at the engine facility. The building in the background is the Philadelphia Museum of Art.
AEM-7 906 brings a passenger train past 30th Street Station. Between 1980 and 1988, Amtrak received 52 of the 7000 hp. electric engines, which are a Swedish design and were built by EMD.

F40PH's 372 and 294 bring the eastbound Broadway Limited into Altoona, Pa., in September of 1982. The station at the time was a small trailer, about 100 feet east of the lead F40 PH. Since then, a new train and bus station has been built, with a covered walkway across the track. In the background are the ever-present helper sets waiting for the next westbound train that needs help for the climb, which starts as the track leaves Altoona and ends 12 miles away at Gallitzin. Amtrak would discontinue the Broadway Limited in September of 1995, but it brought back another train on the same schedule, naming the new train the Three Rivers.

Norfolk and Western J 611 is at Lorain, Ohio, on August 3, 1986, for a westbound photo run-by on a Norfolk Southern Erie, Pa. to Bellevue, Ohio, round trip. 611 was built at N&W's Roanoke, Va. shops, in May of 1950, and was followed by three more of the passenger 4-8-4's. By the late 1950s, 611 was removed from service when the last of the steam railroads decided to drop the fires from their steam engines and switch to diesels. Restored in the early 1980s, 611 is 110' long, 16' high, and has a weight of 435 tons. With 70" drive wheels, 611 produces 80,000 lbs tractive effort. When Norfolk Southern decided to cut its steam program in late 1994, 611 steamed to Roanoke for the last time.

Ex-VIA Rail FPA4's 6758 and 6764 were at Corry, Pa., next to the old Erie mainline, on May 8, 1999. Owned by the New York and Lake Erie Railroad of Gowanda, NY, the ALCO's were at Corry to run freight and passenger trains to Meadville, Pa. on the ex-Erie line. If the blue were switched to black, the old cab units would look right at home. 6758 actually started out as a FPA2 that had been built with a 12-cylinder 244, 1,600 hp. engine. In 1958, 6758 was rebuilt into a FPA4 with ALCO's new 12-cylinder 251, 1,800 hp. engine that was far superior to the 244. Canadian National would acquire 46 of these passenger train engines from ALCO's Montreal Locomotive Works in 1958-1959. In the late 1970s, they were transferred to VIA Rail, created by the Canadian Government to resume passenger service across Canada.

Pennsy's most famous locomotives had to be the 425 members of the Class K4s Pacific. The 4-6-2's were built between 1914 and 1928 by Baldwin Locamotive Company and at the Juniata Shops in Altoona. The passenger engines had an operating weight of 240 tons, producing 44,460 lb tractive effort, and were capable of 100 mph speeds with their 80" drive wheels. They were among the last type to see service on the railroad, lasting until 1957. 1361 was placed on the Horseshoe Curve and 3750 was sent to the Railroad Museum of Pennsylvania at Strasburg. 1361 is shown at the railroad museum in Altoona, in April 1986, before being restored the first time. The second restoration work was started on the engine at Steamtown, in Scranton, Pa. in the late 1990s. The engine was made a Historic Pennsylvania Landmark, and when the restoration work is complete it will return to Altoona where it was constructed in 1918.

Chesapeake and Ohio's 614 is at Terra Alta, West Virginia, on September 12, 1981. It had run west from Cumberland, Md., and was turned and prepared to return to Cumberland with a Chessie System Safety Express excursion. C&O had twelve 4-8-4's for passenger service, and 614 was the last one built for C & O in 1948, by the Lima Locomotive Works. 614 was restored by Chessie System in 1979. Known as the J3a, the engine weights 435 tons with 74" drive wheels, which produce 80,000 lbs tractive effort. Taken out of service in 1985, the locomotive was restored by Iron House Enterprises and steamed again on August 27, 1996. 614 ran limited schedules in New Jersey through the late 1990s.

Milwaukee Road S3 261 rests in Steamtown's former Lackawanna Yards at Scranton, Pa., on July 22, 1995. 261 received a Lackawanna identity while at Scranton and on this day powered a round-trip excursion between Scranton and Binghamton, N.Y. over Canadian Pacific's ex-"The Route of Phoebe Snow" main line. 261 fits in because Lackawanna had Q4 class 4-8-4's ,which had 74" drive wheels and around 70,000 lbs. tractive effort, like the 261. Milwaukee Road had two SI's, forty S2's, and ten S3 class 4-8-4's, with the last group, #260 to 269, built by ALCO in 1944. Last used on the Milwaukee Road in 1954, 261 went to the National Railroad Museum at Green Bay, Wisconsin, and was restored to service on July 30, 1994.

Steamtown was created in the early 1960s by F. Nelson Blount, who obtained a collection of steam engines near Bellows Falls, Vermont. The collection was moved to Scranton, Pa. in 1984, and in 1986 it became Steamtown National Historic Site. 14 stalls at the former Lackawanna roundhouse have been rebuilt, perform work on Steamtown's engines, and also house a museum. 29 steam engines, ranging from a two- truck 1910 Shay to Union Pacific's 4-8-8-4 4012, can be seen throughout the yards.

To the right, Canadian Pacific's 4-6-2 2317, built in 1923 by the Montreal Locomotive Works, sits at Moscow, on November 3, 1985, after bringing an excursion from Scranton. Moscow is located 13 miles east of Scranton, along the former Delaware, Lackawanna and Western mainline, which ran from Buffalo, N.Y. to Hoboken, N.J.

On July 1 of 1862, President Abraham Lincoln signed the Pacific Railroad Act to build the first Transcontinental Railroad. Eventually, Union Pacific would build west from Omaha, Nebraska, for 1,068 miles and the Central Pacific would build east from Sacramento, California, for 690 miles. They would meet at Promontory Summit, on the north side of the Great Salt Lake in Utah, on May 10, 1869. The Lucin Cutoff across the lake would do away with a short section of the original line, including Promontory Summit, in the 1940s. 1.7 miles of track was re-layed at the summit, along with replicas of Central Pacific's Jupiter and Union Pacific's 110. Run by the National Park Service, the locomotives were ready for the 110th Anniversary of the Golden Spike on May 10 1979. Here, the Jupiter and 110 face each other, on September 22, 1998, as their counterparts did 129 years earlier, connecting the East Coast with the West Coast. As you exit Interstate 15 and head west to reach this remote spot, it's hard to imagine the impact that day had in 1869 on the American West. In a land that once seemed invincible, travel across the continent was now within reach of the average person.

Another portion of the Rio Grande narrow gauge that was saved was the 45-mile Silverton Branch in Colorado, today known as the Durango-Silverton Railroad. Finished in 1882, the line climbs from Durango, at 6520', to Silverton, at 9300', on a ruling grade of 2.5% along the Animas River. On October 12, 1990, class K-36 2-8-2 480 is about 10 miles out of Durango on its climb to Silverton.

Durango and Silverton 473 is southbound at High Line on October 12, 1990. In late 1881, construction crews ran into the Animas Canyon a little over 19 miles north of Durango. A shelf along the canyon wall had to be blasted to make way for the railroad. This portion of the railroad became known as the High Line. 473 is one of ten class K-28 2-8-2's built by ALCO in 1923, having 44" drive wheels, and producing 27,540 lbs. tractive effort. The K-28 class was primarily assigned to passenger service on the Rio Grande.

West Virginia Central Railroad's New Tygart Flyer is five miles east of Elkins, West Virginia, on September 6, 2003, with an excursion train to High Falls. The Western Maryland lives on, as speed-lettered, ex-WM FA2 303, ex-Clinchfield F7B 415, and ex-WM BL2 82 head east on the former WM Webster Springs line.

A Burlington Northern Santa Fe Railway DASH8-40CW, SD75M, DASH9-44CW, SD75M engine set brings a westbound trailer train down grade at Tehachapi Loop on October 1, 1997.

A mix of seven GE's and GM's has just passed through Meyersdale, Pa., and are about to pass under the old Western Maryland Salisbury Viaduct with a westbound train, on September 14, 2004. The two ex-Conrail GE's will eventually be repainted into CSX colors. The ex-Burlington Northern SD40-2 and two GM's behind the CSX engines are leased units.

BNSF ex-Santa Fe GP20 3035 is westbound on a double-stack train ten miles east of Marias Pass Summit, on September 20, 1997. Introduced in 1959, GM built 260 GP20s powered by a turbo charged V-16 567D2. Santa Fe would receive 75 of the 2000 hp. locomotives in 1960 through 1961. GM's tapered nose would disappear with the introduction of the GP30. Great Northern would acquire 36 GP20s with a totally different look. They were set up to operate long hood forward, and had a high short hood.

The next two photos offer a slight detour. A trip to Australia, in 1987, would include a three-day ride on the Indian Pacific passenger train form Sydney, on the Pacific Ocean, west 2700 miles across the states of New South Wales, South Australia, and Western Australia to Perth, located on the west coast along the Indian Ocean. At Port Pirie, the train changed its course and turned south to Adelaide, in the southern part of the state of South Australia. Then, the train returned north to Port Pirie, then west to Perth. Between Ooldea and Nurina, the train crossed the world's longest straight section of railroad, 298 miles. As the train left Adelaide, on September 11, 1987, it passed two Australian National Railway GM locomotives built under license in Australia. The country has 26,000 miles of track, with the majority being standard gauge 4' 8 ½" wide.

A trip to New Zealand in 1992 would have me taking a train from Auckland, located near the top of the North Island, south to Wellington. From here, a boat crossed the Cook Strait to Picton, on the northern tip of the South Island. Another southbound train took me to Dunedin, located near the bottom of the island. On November 9, 1992, I took the Taieri Gorge Limited excursion train from Dunedin west 40 miles to Middlemarch. At one time the line continued west to Cromwell. The train stopped several times for photo run-bys, and, as shown heading westbound, was powered by a DJ class diesel. New Zealand Railways operates 2500 miles of 3' 6" gauge track on the North and South Islands.

A mixed, westbound train wraps itself around Horseshoe Curve in central Pennsylvania, as SD40 helpers (former B&O and New Jersey Central) 6289 and 6287 keep the slack bunched up against (sorry Pennsy fans) an ex-New York Central bay window caboose, in April 1985.

Despite being blurred (from the combination of a slow shutter setting to compensate for low light, and the speed of the train) I've always liked this photo of B&O GP30 6938 southbound four miles south of Mt. Jewett, Pa. In September 1972, Chessie System unveiled their new paint scheme, bringing a welcome change from many railroads' somber colors. As they did in the early 1970s, in a sea of bankrupt northeast railroads, the clean fresh colors of these five EMD's brighten up a rainy overcast early afternoon, in August 1986.

My buddies, who would accompanied me on my local trips, Jeff until 1982, and George until October 1991, wait one mile south of Sheffield Jct., along the B&O's Mt. Jewett to Knox branch line, in June 1981. George looks to the left, probably wondering when this show will hit the road. Jeff, on the other hand, after years of playing the waiting game, has accepted the fact that, hey pal, we are not going anywhere until the steel giant shows.

Two Burlinton Northern SD45`s and a B30-7A are on a westbound train at East Glacier, Montana on June 14, 1984. 6502 was delivered to the railroad in 1971. BN would eventually wind up with around 192 SD45's on its roster.

When Conrail quit operations on the former Pennsylvania Railroad's Erie, Pa. to Emporium, Pa. line in 1982, local industries came together to create the Irvine, Johnsonburg, Kane & Warren Railroad, to operate between these towns. Power for this line and the Knox & Kane Railroad was ex-Chessie System GP9 6414 (former Western Maryland 39), built in 1957, and Gettysburg Railroad's RS3 1555 (ex-Long Island Railroad 1555), built in 1955. The pair make an interesting locomotive set as they power an eastbound train through Sheffield, Pa., in late March 1983.

Five miles east of Seligman, Az., on April 26, 1995, SD45 5436 brings a mixed train westbound. Santa Fe would also jump on the SD45 bandwagon acquiring125 between 1966 and 1970.

What image of railroading could be more synonymous with the American Southwest than the Santa Fe Warbonnet? Early morning light reflects off the side of Santa Fe DASH8-40CW 907 as it brings a westbound train downhill at Topock, Az., on April 24, 1995. Within a half mile, the train will cross the Colorado River and proceed into California.

BNSF DASH9-44CW 607 leads a westbound trailer train east of Seligman, Az., on October 4, 1997.

The sun is setting, on October 4, 1997, and soon the Santa Fe red, silver, and yellow image will, too, as BNSF DASH8-40CW 807 heads eastbound, with a double-stack container train, ten miles east of Flagstaff, Az.

Observed from U. S. Route 66, about three miles east of Kingman, Az., a DASH8-40BW, GP60B, GP60M, C30-7 locomotive set powers an eastbound Santa Fe train, on April 26, 1995.

A westbound Union Pacific train crosses the ex-Western Pacific Keddie Wye Bridge, on April 30,1995. The third engine back is Union Pacific's SD40-2 3300 painted for the United Way. Above the second Schneider trailer on the train is the tunnel entrance leading to the connection to the line to Bieber, forming the Keddie Wye.

Delaware-Lackawanna Railroad's C425 2452 is at Scranton, Pa., on July 22, 1995. Created in 1993, the railroad operates ex-Delaware and Hudson and ex-Lackawanna trackage in the Scranton area. Powered by a 16-cylinder, 251C, 2500 hp. engine, ALCO built 91 C425's from May 1964 to the end of 1966. 2452 was one of twelve built for Erie Lackawanna in May 1964. In May 1976, the twelve were sold to the British Columbia Railway. Nineteen years later, 2452 was back at Scranton on home rails and repainted with Erie Lackawanna-inspired colors.

Along with the traffic surge in the 1990s came orders for new locomotives, putting GE and GM beyond capacity at their facilities. GE had a temporary paint building set up at Corry, Pa. The Allegheny & Eastern Railroad would bring the new locomotives to Corry in primer paint and take the newly painted locomotives back to GE. On November 12, 1999, BNSF DASH9-44CW 4576 was at Corry waiting for a train to Erie.

I'm operating Western Pacific F7 921-D at the Portola Railroad Museum, on September 8, 1993. Built for the WP in 1950, the 1500 hp. locomotive was rebuilt at the railroad's Stockton, Ca. shops in the spring of 1978. Union Pacific would donate 921-D to the Feather River Rail Society, at Portola, Ca., on August 26, 1983.

Chapter 9
Knox and Kane Railroad

My dad took this photo of a B&O wooden caboose, Class I-10 C-2644, by the Marienville station in the spring of 1975. At 52 years old, it would be replaced by bay window cabooses within a year. C-2644 was part of an order built (numbers 265 through 314) for the Buffalo, Rochester & Pittsburgh Railway by Standard Steel Car of Butler, Pa. Completed in November 1923, the caboose was originally numbered 293.
When the B&O acquired the BR&P, this group, plus one built in 1914 at the railroad's shops in Dubois, number 150, and numbers 250 through 264 built by Mt. Vernon Car Company at Mt. Vernon, Ill, in 1918 became B & O's class I-10 cabooses. By 1977 the last of these steel under-frame, center-cupola cabooses would be taken out of service.

In May 1980, B&O GP9 6445 and a C&O GP9 haul a northbound train on the Knox, Pa. to Mt. Jewett, Pa. branch line at Chaffee. Originally built as a narrow gauge by the Pittsburgh, Bradford and Buffalo Railroad in the early 1880s, the line connected with the Pittsburgh and Western at Foxburg, Pa. with through service to Pittsburgh. Chessie operated the line until 1982, when Sloan Cornell bought the line and operated as the Knox and Kane Railroad.

In 1987 excursion trains were started over the line from Marienville to the former Erie Railroad, 2053' long, 301' high Kinzua Bridge. Four miles of track had to be re-laid from Mt. Jewett north to reach the bridge. At first, diesels would haul the train from Marienville to Kane, where ex-Huntington and Broad Top Railroad's 1927 Baldwin 2-8-0 38 would take the train to the Kinzua Bridge and back to Kane, where the diesels would return the train to Marienville. In 1990, a new SY Class 2-8-2, built at the Tangshan Shops in China in 1989, arrived and powered the trains round trip from Marienville. The six-year-old 58 is northbound between Russell City and Nansen, on October 12, 1995.

Rail photography can be challenging, with changing light conditions and sometimes unpredictable schedule of trains. Sometimes things work out and make the effort worthwhile. On June 19, 1994, 58 could be heard blowing for the Rt. 66 grade crossing at Nansen with a southbound excursion train. With a downhill run to Russell City, and not working any steam, 58 drifts into view five minutes later. In a way, the Knox & Kane Railroad gives one a link to the past, indicating what railroading was like at the early part of the 20th century. 58 could easily pass for a B&O engine working the line back in the 1920s.

The Kinzua Bridge was construction between 1881 and 1882 with 3,100,000 lbs. of wrought iron; at the time it was the world's highest railroad bridge, at 301'. For the ever-increasing train weights, the bridge was rebuilt in 1900 with 6,700,000 lbs. of steel. The Erie Railroad had built south from Salamanca, N.Y. in 1859, to reach the coal fields south of Bradford, Pa. Once these fields were mined out, the Erie started building south from Crawford Junction toward Mt. Jewett, Pa. Faced with the choice of building many miles of track with steep grades to run down the Kinzua Valley and back up the other side, a bridge seemed the obvious solution. By 1958 traffic levels on the line weren't enough to justify maintaining the bridge and Erie switched to the B&O's track between Howard Junction (south of Bradford) to Mt. Jewett. The last Erie train over the bridge was an excursion train, on June 21, 1959. The bridge was saved from being torn down in 1963 when a Pennsylvania bill was signed establishing the Kinzua Bridge State Park. On August 7, 1987, 2-8-0 38 would haul the first excursion train over the reopened bridge. The photo shows engine 38 with a train passing over the bridge, on October 25, 1987.

Standing on the top of the two-level open car, on August 16, 1987, provided a good view of 38 slowly running across the bridge. The road at the bottom was at one time the Kushequa Railroad, built in 1898 to haul logs to the Kushequa Saw Mill located a mile and a half to the west of the bridge.

The bridge is seen from the cab of GP9 39 as the train starts its trip back to Marienville, on June 8, 2001. The GP9 started out on the "Fast Freight Line" as 39. It was renumbered 6414 on Chessie System, 14 on the Knox and Kane Railroad, and would be sent to the Gettysburg Railroad operated by Sloan Cornell. When the Gettysburg line was sold, it came back to the Knox and Kane Railroad in 1997, with its original number, 39.

Knox and Kane's "One Spot" hauls a southbound train one mile south of Watson Farm, in August 1988. Built by Porter in 1945, the 50 ton, 300 hp. switcher looks like a cross between a stream engine and a diesel, with its steam-era pilot and side rods. The light engine, with its ability to handle only three or four cars, was soon replaced on the excursion trains.

44 brings a southbound train through Sheffield Junction, on August 20, 1989. The S6, 900 hp. switcher was built by ALCO in 1957 for the South Buffalo Railway. I'm standing on the abandoned Tionesta Valley Railway grade, where to the right and out of the photo there was a diamond where the narrow gauge line crossed the B&O.

Hagerstown chop-nose GP9 39 is Kinzua Bridge-bound, one mile north of Pigeon, Pa., on June 28, 1997. When the Knox and Kane Railroad started, they acquired this engine from Chessie System to operate this line, and the former Pennsy line between Johnsonburg, Warren, and Irvine, which later became part of the Allegheny Railroad. 39 was built in 1957 and was one of 21 GP9's built for the Western Maryland Railway between 1954 and 1957. To increase visibility, all of the GP9's and Western Maryland's four GP7's would have their short, high hoods chopped down, starting in the early 1960s at WM's Hagerstown, Maryland, shops.

Who would have thought that eight years after Chessie System filed to abandon the line, a new steam engine would be operating passenger trains on a regular schedule five months out of the year over this route. Engine 58 started operating on this line in early June of 1990. A relatively small engine, 58 has an operating weight of 143 tons and produces 38,130 lbs of tractive effort, with its 54" drive wheels. It is ideally suited for the 85 lb. and 100 lb. rails on the line. This photo shows 58 northbound near Pigeon, on October 20, 1991.

Below, 58 is southbound with a train near the top of the Byramtown hill, on August 2, 1992.

Engine 58 moves northbound with a fourteen-car train, one mile south of Sheffield Junction, on October 29, 1995. The SY Class was intended for industrial service. With a production run from 1969 to 1999, around 1700 were built by Tangshan Locomotive Works, based on a 1920s ALCO design.

The 58 is pouring on the coal as it brings a heavy northbound train uphill, two miles south of Watson Farm, on October 3, 1992.

58 had only been in service a little over two weeks as it ran a northbound train near Pigeon, on June 16, 1990.

Both 58 and 39 work a fourteen-car train northbound near Pigeon, on October 24, 1998.

When Knox and Kane started excursion trains to the Kinzua Bridge in 1987, the wye at the north end of the bridge had not been completed. 2-8-0 38 is shown unhooking from the train after running in reverse from Kane, on August 16, 1987.

Porter #1 waits for engine 38 to run into the siding, then moves ahead to couple to the train, and pulling it back clear of the siding. 38 then pulls back onto the bridge, and recouples to the opposite end of the train for the return trip to Kane.

As the train heads south over Kinzua Bridge, the little Porter will follow the train to Mt. Jewett.

58 and 44 are double-heading a fourteen-car excursion train coming into Watson Farm, on October 16, 1994. From the fireman's seat, the S6's six-cylinder, 251B engine appears to be putting out more smoke than 58, as both engines are working hard to bring the train uphill through an s-curve northbound.

58 climbs up the grade near the top of Chaffee Hill, with an early season, southbound excursion train, on June 6, 1992.

On most occasions when the train would double head, the helper would cut off the northbound train at Mt.Jewett, leaving 58 to take the train to Kinzua Bridge, and then go back to Marienville. 58 is shown running southbound, passing 44 at Mt. Jewett, on October 16, 1994. When 58 passed, the ALCO switcher would follow the train back to Marienville.

Winter isn't far ahead, as 58 is northbound, on October 26, 1991, about one and one half miles south of Russell City. Overnight accommodations in a caboose could be had at Kinzua Bridge.

At Marienville, a caboose would be added to the train, and dropped off at a short siding just south of the bridge. The next day's train would return the caboose to Marienville. Here, an ex-Pennsylvania Railroad N8 caboose brings up the rear of the northbound train. It's Pennsy high-iron days are long gone as the old cabin car rolls along the 90-year-old, 85 lb. rail, at 15 mph.

Snow and steam engines always seem to make a good combination for photography. 58 is northbound with the last train of the season, one mile north of Pigeon, on a snowy October 31, 1993.

On October 5, 1990, 58 is southbound at the Route 948 crossing at Chaffee. From here, the train would start climbing Chaffee Hill. Although less then a mile long, the steep and curvy climb would always give the 58 with a big train a good workout.

58 and 44 are northbound at the Sheffield Junction hill, on October 17, 1992. The abandoned Tionesta Valley Railway's grade to Brookston is just off to the left of the train. The T.V.R.Y. had beat the Pittsburgh, Bradford & Buffalo Railroad to Sheffield Junction (that is around the curve behind the train here) by a few months, in 1882. Pittsburgh & Western would later gain control of the PB&B Railroad; then the Bradford, Bordell & Kinzua Railroad leased the line from Mt. Jewett to Foxburg. B. & O., which had a controlling interest of the Pittsburg & Western, took over operations on the line from Kane south to Pittsburgh in 1902, and from Kane to Mt. Jewett in 1906. B. & O. standard-gauged the line in October 1911. Passenger trains operated until January 1933 and mixed passenger trains until 1937. The T.V.R.Y. narrow gauge lines would eventually total around 300 miles. From Sheffield, the mainline ran south to Hallton on the Clarion River. Lines also ran north of Sheffield, and a spider-web of logging branch lines supplied logs to the Sheffield mills for 60 years.

Engine 58 heads for the Kinzua Bridge, one mile north of Pigeon, on August 17, 1999. The Pennsy caboose adds a nice touch to the end of the train.

From mid-September through the end of October, activity was always interesting on the Knox and Kane. Engine 58 could easily be heard a half-hour in advance, with a long northbound train. Even with a helper, 58 would loose its footing on the numerous curves and grades where difficulty could be compounded by leaves and wet rail. On a picture-perfect day, October 11, 1998, the fall colors were at their peak as 58 moved southbound on top of Sheffield Junction hill. 39 was running light about one mile behind.

58 and 39 are northbound with another big train, one mile south of Russell City, on October 18, 1998. With most of the foliage gone, this time of year was good for getting photos of the train at locations that were totally surrounded by shade on sunny summer days. In late June of 2002, the Kinzua Bridge was closed to the excursion trains, then to pedestrians in August. Last painted by the Erie Railroad in the early 1950s, years of neglect had caught up with the bridge. Over 10 million dollars was secured for rebuilding and paint, that would allow trains and people out on the bridge again. Rebuilding started in early 2003, with six towers on the Mt. Jewett side, and three towers on the north side completed by July. On July 21, 2003, a 100-mph tornado hit the bridge, causing the eleven un-rebuilt towers to collapse. At the time of this writing, the fate of the bridge is still uncertain, with rebuilding costs estimated at 45 million dollars.

58 was between Russell City and Nansen with a northbound train, on September 30, 2001. Not knowing it at the time, this would be 58's last year of regular service over the line. In 2002, the locomotive operated once north and south over the line. I'm not sure when the B & O dieselized the line, possibly by the mid-1950s. Amazingly, after a gap of nearly forty years, starting in 1990 for twelve years, steam would return from Kane south to Marienville.

Knox and Kane Railroad engine RS36 70 (ex-Nickel Plate Road 870, ex-Norfolk and Western 2870) headed north with an excursion train just past Sheffield Junction on the way to Kinzua Bridge, on June 16, 2000. 70 was built for the Nickel Plate Road in 1962, and its 1800 hp., 251C V-12 engine performed one of ALCO's characteristic trademarks of turning diesel fuel into smoke. 70 came to the Knox and Kane Railroad in 1997 from the Gettysburg Railroad. With ALCO's turbochargers being driven by exhaust gases, the advancement of the throttle feeds more fuel into the cylinders, causing turbo lag until the cylinder pressure increases enough to drive the turbocharger faster. The incomplete combustion of fuel is the end result, which gives ALCO's honorary steam locomotive black smoke. ALCO's 241, 244, and 251 engines have a 668-cubic inch displacement per cylinder. In the 1950s, the 251 V-12 produced roughly the same horsepower as GM's V-16 567, but with better fuel economy and four fewer cylinders to maintain.

Of my interest in railroads over the years, people would always ask me, "Why?". Maybe this shot, taken by my dad in March 1978, will explain. The sights and sounds of railroading come alive as the diesel exhaust of four idling GP9's penetrate the air. In the background, the remains of a B&O wagon-top boxcar serves as a storage shed, while on the left is a B&O wooded caboose, and the Marienville station is the right. Growing up along this line, how could one not develop an interest in railroads, and especially in the B&O's that had been in existence for 150 years at the time of this photo? Here, the Jordan Spreader was brought in to clear the line after heavy snows hit the area in January and February.

On February 10, 2003, RS36 70 was bringing four cars north at Watson Farm. Because of an ice build-up at the crossing, 70 would uncouple from the cars, pass through the crossing, then recouple to the cars, and proceed to the next crossing and repeat the process. Even with rails being chipped clear by the track crew, 70 would derail the front truck at the first crossing north of Watson Farm. By late the following morning, with the help of jacks and a pull on a cable from a bulldozer on the right side, the locomotive was back on the rails. In true ALCO fashion, engine 70 smokes it up as it makes another try at the crossing. The front truck would make it, but one axle on the back truck would derail. Within an hour, 70 would be back on track, recoupled to the cars, and northbound to the next crossing.

70 was northbound at Nansen, on October 16, 2004, with four boxcars of particle board on a far better day to be railroading. Being built in 1962, it was somewhat surprising to see 70 equipped with pole pockets on the front and back of the frame.

GP9 39 splits the crossing signs running B & O style with a Kinzua Bridge-bound train, one mile north of Sheffield Junction, on August 1, 2002.

At the beginning of the operating season, Knox and Kane would place a concession car on a short siding at the south end of the Kinzua Bridge. The last train of the season, or the helper engine, would pick up the car and return it to Marienville. 58 has just passed southbound, on October 29, 1995, shortly followed by 44 with the concession car near the top of Chaffee Hill.

In early August of 1992, 58 would have a run-in with a truck at the Lantz Corners crossing on Route 219. Knox and Kane turned to the Allegheny Railroad and borrowed their CF7 104 for a week. The 104 was a surprise to see as it powered a northbound train one mile north of Pigeon, on August 9, 1992.

At the same location as the CF7, Porter #1 brings its maximum tonnage train northbound, on June 11, 1988. As much as I miss the B&O days on the Mt. Jewett to Knox branch, one has to appreciate the interesting chapter the Knox and Kane Railroad has left on the history of this line.

Chapter 10
Allegheny Railroad
(Allegheny & Eastern Railroad)

At one time the Pennsylvania Railroad operated this line. Part of Pennsy's Northern Region from Erie, it ran 150 miles east to Emporium where it joined the Buffalo-Harrisburg mainline. Originally the Philadelphia and Erie Railroad, the Pennsy leased the line after they financed the completion of the line to Erie in 1864. By the end of 1982, Conrail stopped operating the line, and local industries in Warren purchased the section from Johnsonburg, were it connected with the Chessie System to Warren and Irvine. Sloan Cornell operated the line until the Hammermill Paper Company acquired the 150 mile line, creating Allegheny Railroad. In 1992, the railroad was acquired by Genesee and Wyoming Industries, and it was renamed Allegheny and Eastern Railroad. The Allegheny & Eastern was merged into the Buffalo & Pittsburgh Railroad in 2004.

Two Bessemer & Lake Erie (B&LE) SD9's were leased to help with track work in 1986. Here, at the Kane Station, 843 rests with Allegheny's ex-Santa Fe CF7 2590. The B&LE operated 205 miles of track from North Bessemer and reached the Lake Erie harbors of Conneaut, Ohio, and Erie, Pa. Mainly built to haul raw materials to the Pittsburgh steel mills,"The Bessemer Route" was hit hard by the declining steel industry. Canadian National took over operations of the B&LE, in May of 2004.

GP40's 101 and 102 (ex-Penn Central 3242, and 3251 built in 1968) proceeding eastbound are about to pass under the Knox and Kane Railroad at Kane, on March 23, 1989. Power for the line was provided by these two GP40s, three ex-Santa Fe CF7's, and two ex-Union Pacific GP35's.

GP40s 101, 102, and CF7 104 are on an eastbound train, one mile from Roystone, on January 14, 1989. With a harbor at Erie, this line was an important route for moving iron ore to the steel mills in eastern Pennsylvania. Forty years before, this scene might have been two class I 2-10-0's on the head end of the loaded ore train, with two more shoving against an N5 caboose. The Kane Hill required helpers from Warren east to Kane, and Ridgway west to Kane. Helpers would also be needed at Ridgway on eastbound trains to St. Mary's.

Chapter 11
Baltimore & Ohio, Chessie System, and Buffalo and Pittsburgh Railroad

"Linking 13 Great States with the Nation," the Baltimore & Ohio was America's first common carrier railroad, charted in 1827. By the time the Chessie System and Seaboard System were officially merged in 1987, the B & O had been in existence 160 years. How many other companies in the United States could claim that record? What more could symbolize northeastern railroading in the 1960s and 1970s than B & O Blue GP9's, set up to operate long hood forward, hauling a load of "black diamonds" out of the coal fields?

GP9 6546 led a train northbound at Watson Farm, Pa., in July of 1978. The coal was loaded in Clarion County and hauled to B & O's Buffalo Division mainline, at Mt. Jewett, Pa.

Along the Buffalo Division mainline, two miles north of Mt. Jewett, GP30 6960 leads a long southbound train, on April 14, 1985. At the time of this photo, the Capital Dome GP30 had been on the B & O for 23 years. An order for 77 of these 2250 hp. engines were delivered to the railroad from late 1962 through early 1963.

GP40 3768, SD35 7414, and a WM GP9 haul a westbound train through Terra Alta, W. Va., on September 12, 1981. This mainline left the Baltimore to Chicago mainline at Cumberland, Md., and at the time of this photo ran west to St. Louis, Mo. In the background can be seen the passenger cars of the Chessie System Safety Express, powered by 4-8-4 614, shown earlier in this book. (See p. 112.)

At Ridgway Pa., B&O GP40-2 4337 leads a southbound train, in November of 1985. To the far right of the train, a derailment occurred here, on November 4, 1944. A northbound passenger train was slowing for a stop at the Ridgway station when the Class P-18-A 4-6-2 struck an automobile and derailed. The engine rolled on to its side and was blocking the southbound main. Moments later, a southbound freight train powered by Class LL 2-6-6-2 7534 came around the curve and was unable to stop in time to avoid the collision. The engine and thirteen cars of the ninety-four-car train derailed, killing the fireman.

In the mid-1980s, Sea Land double-stack container trains started running over the Buffalo Division. The Susquehanna Railroad would run the train from Little Ferry, N.J., with trackage rights on Conrail to Buffalo, N.Y. Because of clearance restrictions on Conrail and Norfolk Southern west of Buffalo, the trains were forced to run south to Pittsburgh. From Pittsburgh, Chessie System would haul the train to Chicago, where Burlington Northern would take over and run the train to the Pacific Northwest. After 1989 the clearances west of Buffalo were improved, and the double-stacks switched to the shorter routes. On November 30, 1986, B&O SD40 7592 and two other six-axle GM's rolled a southbound double-stack train two miles north of Mt. Jewett.

Since B &O's arrival in 1842, Cumberland, Maryland, was to B&O what Altoona, Pennsylvania, had been to the Pennsy. Maintaining equipment had always been part of the scene at Cumberland, and so it continues to this day as CSX's major locomotive rebuild center. In 1966, B&O received its first 3000 hp. GP40s. They preformed well from long-distance trailer and container trains to mine runs. Eventually, 161 GP40's and 216 GP40-2's were added to the roster. Here, on September 12, 1981, GP40-2 4205 and GP38 3839 leave Cumberland with a westbound train. On the adjacent track is SD7 1827. Five of these six-axle, 1500 hp. EMD's arrived on the railroad from 1952 through 1953.

B&O SD7 1827 was at Cumberland, Md., on September 12,1981. Lacking dynamic brakes, the locomotive spent most of the time in yard work, where its six traction motors were put to use switching large cuts of cars. Introduced in 1951, the SD7 was a stretched version of the GP7. The two extra sets of wheels gave the locomotive a reduced axle loading, ideal for branchlines with less damage to the lighter bridges and rails.

B&O GP40 3690 was proceeding southbound, five miles north of Du Bois, Pa., in August of 1985. The last engine is Western Maryland 3576, the first of five GP35's received by the Western Maryland in 1963.

C&O GP30 3018, B&O GP38 3837, and two B&O GP40-2's were going southbound with a Sea Land, double-stack train three miles south of Mt. Jewett, on May 25, 1986. A wide, flat, open area and the telephone poles curving to the right indicate that at one time this location contained a small yard.

In August of 1980, B&O GP40-2 1977 and B&O GP40 3768 were both at rest at Mt. Jewett. Engine 1977 was the second GP40-2 to be numbered for B&O's 150th anniversary (1827-1977). The first engine having the number was put on display with the new Chessie System paint scheme, but was shortly renumbered to 4100. The 1977 would carry the number from 1972 to 1984, when it was renumbered to 4163. It would be interesting to know if GP40-2 1977 and SD7 1827 were ever paired together.

B&O GP40-2 4110 brings an unusual train northbound two miles north of Mt. Jewett in April 1986. The Government of Ontario Transit commuter cars head toward Toronto, possibly having been on loan to another transit line to the south.

The end of an era was passing as C&O extended-vision-cupola caboose 903253 brought up the end of a northbound train, two miles north of Mt. Jewett, on December 14, 1986. The waving hand from a person in a caboose would be replaced with a red, flashing light of a "FRED," attached to the coupler of the last freight car.

At around 2,200 feet in elevation, the winters at Mt. Jewett always appear to be colder and the winds are seemingly unending. The cold wait pays off here as C&O SD40 7504, C&O GP30 3009, and an ex-Seaboard Coast Line GP40 power a northbound Sea Land double-stack train, two miles north of Mt. Jewett, on December 14, 1986. Chessie System would be gone within a year, and the stack trains were switched to shorter routes by the end of the 1980s.

Chesapeake and Ohio GP9 6011 was at Bradford, Pa. in September of 1980. B&O kept an engine here to switch for the Kendall Oil Refinery and other industries in the area.

A northbound train passes through the Bradford, Pa. area, in late August of 1980, powered by B&O GP30 6969, B&O GP40-2 4250, C&O SD35 7431, and B&O GP38 3828. In the steam days, helpers would be added to southbound trains at Bradford for the 1.5%, eight-mile climb up Bingham Hill.

After the creation of Chessie System, the old Buffalo Division could be mistaken for a line on "George Washington's Railroad," with all the Chesapeake & Ohio engines and cabooses operating over the line. Here, on May 25, 1986, GP30 3018 hauls a southbound Sea Land stack train at Johnsonburg, Pa. Like the B&O, C&O had a sizable fleet of 48 GP30s delivered to the railroad in 1963, with road numbers 3000 trough 3047.

On April 26, 1987, C&O SD50 8564 was on a northbound train, two miles north of Mt Jewett. The SD50s turned out to be the last engines ordered by Chessie System. EMD delivered 63 of the 3500 hp. (later 3600 hp) engines between February 1984 and November 1985, with C&O receiving 43 and B&O receiving 20. My dog George gives the train a roll-by inspection.

B&O wasn't a GE customer, but after the merges in the 1970s and 1980s, GE engines would show up on occasion. On June 19, 1988, the unmistakable chugging sound of a GE on a northbound train coming into Mt. Jewett could be heard. Two miles later, CSX 7205 (ex-Louisville & Nashville 1475, ex-Seaboard System 7205) passed with a Sea Land stack train. The engine was one of 78 U3OC's built for "The Dixie Line" between 1969 and 1972. The 3000 hp., six-axle engines turned out to be GE's most successful Universal Series locomotive, with 600 of the "U-Boats" built for 21 railroads between 1966 and 1976.

At one time, the Buffalo Division was the Buffalo Rochester & Pittsburgh (BR&P) Railway (incorporated in 1887), which operated 600 miles of track between it's namesake cities. In 1932, B&O acquired control of the BR&P. The next owner, CSX, sold the line to Genesee and Wyoming Industries, on July 19, 1988, to create today's Buffalo and Pittsburgh Railroad (B&P). These two photos were taken on August 28, 1988, a month after B&P started up. In the first photo, leased CSX GP38 2068 led a Sea Land double-stack train southbound, two miles north of Mt. Jewett. In the second photo, GP40 6521 and GP40-2 6111 had been added to the train, and are shown five miles south of Mt. Jewett.

On October 2, 1994, CSX SD40-2 8229 and C30-7 7036 hauled an empty coal train southbound, three miles north of Mt. Jewett. At the time, this portion of the line had one northbound and one southbound train a day, with an occasional unit coal train and a local train to serve local industries.

GP40 3111 ran southbound, two miles north of Mt. Jewett, on July 10, 1993. B&P acquired six of the former New York Central engines from the Kyle Railroad. By the late 1990s, the B&P was an all-EMD railroad, with five GP9's, two GP18's, six GP38's, fifteen GP40's, and eight SD45's.

When Allegheny & Eastern (A&E) became part of Genesee & Wyoming Industries in 1992, its engines could be seen regularly on the B&P lines. On October 17, 1997, A&E 306 and three SD45's were on a southbound train, three miles north of Mt. Jewett. The GP35 started out as Union Pacific #748; Union Pacific had received 24 of the 2500 hp. locomotives from GM between 1963 and 1964. Despite its 33 years of road service, the engine still appeared to be in good operating condition.

Allegheny & Eastern GP40 302 and six more four-axle GM's are northbound on a loaded, 100-car, coal train at Hutchins, on September 25 1995. Between Johnsonburg and Mt. Jewett, northbound trains have the 11-mile, 1% Clarion Hill to climb. B.R.&P acquired nine XX Class 2-8-8-2's between 1918 and 1923, and they were assigned as helpers for this hill. Built by ALCO's Brooks Shops, at 102 feet in length, 285 tons, and producing 113,000 tractive effort, these were B.R.&P's largest locomotives. By 1952 they were taken out of service by B&O.

B&P's diesels were all with four axles, but for the heavy coal trains larger power was needed. In late 1995, B&P acquired eight ex-Southern Pacific SD45's from Helm Leasing. These engines were B&P's first six-axle power. On July 14, 1996, three SD45's were on a southbound train, four miles south of Mt. Jewett.

Three miles north of Mt. Jewett, on March 12, 1996, three SD45's headed a southbound train. B&P and other smaller railroads were priced out of the new locomotive market, and had to rely on rebuilt four- and six-axle power. With the sameness of the newer GM's and GE's running on the bigger railroads, these SD45's gave the Buffalo and Pittsburgh Railroad a 1960s-era look.

After the Erie Railroad built the Kinzua Bridge, its rails reached Mt. Jewett and continued south to Clarion Junction, near Johnsonburg. From there the Erie used the Pennsylvania Railroad (Philadelphia and Erie) to Ridgway, where they continued to Brockway on the Ridgway & Clearfield Railroad. The Rochester and Pittsburgh (later Buffalo, Rochester & Pittsburgh) had built a line south, from Rochester through Bradford to Howard Junction. From there the R&P arranged for trackage rights over the Erie for 38 miles to Clarion Junction, where they would continue south towards Pittsburgh on their own rails. Due to traffic congestion on the single track Erie line, BR&P constructed a line north, from Mt. Jewett to Howard Junction, to bypass the Kinzua Bridge. South of Mt. Jewett, the line was double- tracked, and both railroads continued to operate over the line. With the rebuilding of the BR&P south of Johnsonburg, the Erie switched from the Pennsy to the BR&P to get to Brockway. When the last Erie Lackawanna train ran, on April 1, 1976, the track from Clarion Junction to Mt. Jewett was transferred to Chessie System.

The railroads known for "Safety and Service" and "Serving the Heart of Industrial America" were long-gone when GP38 2001 led a southbound train, four miles south of Mt. Jewett, on October 23, 1994.

One-half mile farther south, SD45 457 brought a southbound train near Hutchins, on April 21, 1996. In reality, 457 is an SD40-2 with a 16-cylinder, 3000 hp. engine, but it retained its SD45 body.

B&O's unmistakable, color-position light signals gave away the line's former owner, but by the 1990s the old Buffalo Division had taken on a new look. Instead of B&O, Chessie System, and CSX colors, the Buffalo and Pittsburgh Railroad's orange, black, and yellow diesels now powered the trains. In this photo GP38 2000 (ex-Baltimore and Ohio 3837 built in 1967) leads a southbound train two miles north of Mt. Jewett, on March 2, 1996. The ex-CSX engine and trailing GP38 2001 (ex-Louisville and Nashville, built in 1970) were rebuilt in 1994. Their non-turbocharged, 645E, V-16 engines produce 2000 hp.

Most of B&P trains through Mt Jewett after early 1996 were powered by the eight, ex-Southern Pacific, SD45's. The engines were known for poor fuel economy, and the longer crankshafts were more prone to breakage. Despite these set backs, over 1700 SD45's of various models were built over a ten-year period.

At the time the following photos were taken, the engines had been in heavy mainline service for thirty years. They started with Southern Pacific hauling freight, from New Orleans across the southwest to Los Angeles, up through the Pacific Northwest to Portland, Oregon, and from the San Francisco Bay area through Donner Pass to Ogden, Utah. They also ran through on other railroads, racking up millions of miles apiece. Having just been rebuilt, these engines look like they just rolled out of La Grange. Now on the 370-mile, regional B&P line, they were still doing what GM designed them to do: moving thousands of tons of freight at a fraction of the cost of a truck on a highway.

SD45 457 leads two others and a GP40 on a southbound train, four miles north of Mt. Jewett, on June 12, 1996.

SD45 451 leans into a curve at 40mph, with 100-plus cars on a southbound train, three miles north of Mt. Jewett, on June 20, 1998. The SD45 was one EMD model that the B&O failed to acquire.

In early B&P days, six engines were on a southbound train, three miles north of Mt. Jewett, on September 25,1988. The hodge-podge of power, starting from B&O boxcar 483193, consisted of: CSX (ex-Seaboard System) C30-7 7073, CSX (ex- Seaboard Coast Line) GP40 6671, CSX (ex- B&O) GP40 6607, an unknown B&P GP9, CSX (ex-B&O) GP40-2 6058, and finally CSX (ex-B&O) GP40 6637.

Three miles north of Mt. Jewett, three SD45's and three GP40s were on a southbound train, on May 2, 1996.

Three and one-half miles north of Mt. Jewett, on June 6, 1996, three SD45's bring the daily BNZ southbound through an s-curve.

SD45 454 is moving southbound, on June 26, 1996. Buffalo and Pittsburgh's engines 450 to 457 are part of a group of 167 SD45's that Southern Pacific rebuilt at its Sacramento, Ca. shops between 1979 and 1985. The engines retained their 20-cylinder engines, but were de-rated to 3,200 hp. Classified as SD45R's on the Southern Pacific, B&P listed engines 450 to 456 as SD45-2's, and engine 457 as an SD40-2. For simplicity, I have referred to the eight engines as SD45's.

CSX would sell the Rochester line to Genesee & Wyoming Industries, on July 31, 1986, creating the Rochester and Southern Railroad (R&S). R&S GP40 102 is at the head end of a southbound train, three miles north of Mt. Jewett, on October 4, 1996. Built in 1968 for the New York Central, engine 102 has a slight color variation from the B&P engines, with its silver trucks and fuel tank.

This photo of Buffalo & Pittsburgh SD45's was taken on February 25, 1996, four miles south of Mt. Jewett. Here, three of the big, ex-SP locomotives and an Allegheny & Eastern GP40 302 move southbound with a 100-plus-car train.

The Buffalo & Pittsburgh would take on a new look in 2007. Here, EMLX's (ex-Union Pacific) SD90MAC-H II's 8526, 8530 and 8522 are on a southbound train on the 4 1/2-mile-long straight, just north of Mt. Jewett, on September 24, 2007. These three 6000 hp. locomotives were part of an order for 40 delivered to Union Pacific in 1999. UP would eventually have 62 on its roster. Due to their advanced technology, the locomotives would suffer high out-of-service time. By mid-2007, UP would return 41 to GM Leasing (EMLX), and the remaining 21 were taken out of service. Canadian Pacific would be the only other railroad to acquire the SD90MAC-H II model, with 4 in 2000. GE's 6000 hp., AC6000CW would fare a little better, with 117 going to CSX, 80 to Union Pacific, and 8 to BHP Iron Ore in Australia. The 6000 hp. locomotive sales didn't develop like GM and GE had hoped, since railroads for the time being settled for new locomotives in the 4000 hp. to 4400 hp. range.

At the same location, another southbound train is led by SD90MAC-H II 8526, on October 21, 2007.

The SD90MAC-H II would incorporate several changes over the SD90MAC-H (shown earlier with Union Pacific 8510 on an eastbound coal train at O'Fallon's Nebraska). The most visible change was a new nose design to accommodate a full height door and rectangular windows, giving the new locomotives a boxier look. Other changes were an improved version of the 265H engine, three radiator fans reduced to two, and the rear sandbox redesigned for a more contoured look. The SD90MAC-H II has an overall length of 80' 2" and a weight of 212.5 tons.
The 8530 rounds a bend north of Mt. Jewett with a southbound train, on October 28, 2007. Despite being a large locomotive, the SD45 looks dwarfed sandwiched between the two 90MAC's. 8530's huge flared radiators really stand out, compared to the ones on the SD45.

The same 90-45-90 locomotive set powers a late southbound train 7 miles north of Mt. Jewett, on October 30, 2007. B & P would be leasing six of the 90MAC's in 2007.

On October 31, 2007, a face full of 45's are southbound one mile north of Hutchins. A six-SD45 locomotive set would have been impressive enough in the late 1960s, but other than Montana Rail Link, what other railroad besides B & P could assemble a set in 2007? Even with their 20-cylinder engines derated to 3,200 h.p., there was still 19,200 hp. at the ready in this 395-foot long, 1,092-ton lash up. Other than an updated electrical system, the locomotives were using the same 1960s mechanical technology as when they were built, between 1966 and 1970 for Southern Pacific and their subsidiary, Cotton Belt. It would be interesting if one could calculate the total mileage traveled and tonnage hauled by these six locomotives, in their nearly 240 combined years of road service. As they passed, time, miles, and tonnage continued to be added to the total.

SD90MAC-H II's 8531, 8527 and B & P GP9 626 are heading southbound, four miles north of Mt. Jewett, on February 16, 2008. The size of the big, six-axle locomotives are brought into perspective coupled to the pint-sized GP9.

Recently rebuilt and receiving a chopped nose, GP9 626, ex-Norfolk & Western, built in October 1958, hides its nearly 50 years well. Normally assigned to Bradford for local work, 626 is likely going to B & P's locomotive shop at Butler, Pa. for maintenance or inspection.

SD90MAC-H II 8527 and two SD45's were going southbound, four miles north of Mt. Jewett, on January 8, 2008. Before the train arrived, I was trying to visualize standing here in the 1940s, as ex-BR&P 2-6-6-2's worked trains uphill out of Bradford. Nostalgia is a funny thing, and chances are if the rails are still here in 60 years, someone will be standing at this location waiting for a train, trying to imagine the sights and sounds of SD90MAC's and SD45's bringing another southbound train through, in that long ago year of 2008.

To eleviate traffic congestion on the single track Erie line, B.R. & P. would create the Johnsonburg and Bradford Railroad (J&B), to build about 20 miles of track from Howard Junction south to Mt. Jewett. The single track line opened in June 1893. BR&P would double-track the Erie line from Mt. Jewett south to Clarion Junction in 1894. By 1910, the railroad realigned and double-tracked eight miles of the line, north from Mt. Jewett. With its numerous curves and almost one-mile-longer length, the old abandoned J&B grade crossed the new line at six locations.
115 years had passed since the stone masons placed the 32-inch wide, 18-inch thick, 9-foot combined length end cap stones on the drainage culvert under the abandoned grade north of Mt. Jewett, when this picture was taken on May 11, 2008. Built to withstand many decades of passing trains, this portion of the line would be in operation only 17 years.

On September 14, 2007, north of Mt. Jewett on the 1910 line, three SD45's are working uphill with a 100-car, southbound train. 453 was five months shy of 40 years old, having been built for SP in February 1968. The locomotive's paint is beginning to show the wear and tear of 12 years of service on the B. & P.

8530 and two more SD90MAC-H II's were heading southbound, 3 ½ miles north of Mt. Jewett, on February 24, 2008. Minus their nose shields, and with slashes through Union Pacific, the locomotives are a long way from Sherman Hill, having at least for the time being found a home in western Pennsylvania and New York on the Buffalo & Pittsburgh.

SD90MAC's 8523 and 8530 split the old B&O color position signals, on the long straight north of Mt. Jewett, on July 23, 2008, with a 77-car, southbound train. While the northbound signal is deactivated and turned from the track, the southbound signal is still in use.

A final look at the B&P shows two SD45's and a SD90MAC southbound, coming into the north end of the long straight north of Mt. Jewett, on July 31, 2008. Another SD45 with many years of hard miles, 460's well weathered Southern Pacific gray, along with B&P orange and UP yellow, give an interesting mix of colors. In spite of the low traffic density on the line, the combination of 1960s and 1990s, high horsepower EMD's always makes it worth the trip to spend time along B&P's former Buffalo, Rochester and Pittsburgh Railway's Middle Division.

Chapter 12
ALCO

The American Locomotive Company (ALCO) was formed at Schenectady, N.Y., in 1901, with the merger of nine locomotive manufactures, a Canadian builder in 1904, and the Rogers Locomotive Works in 1905. The Schenectady plant would become the headquarters of the company, originally The Schenectady Locomotive Engine Manufactory, which produced its first locomotive in 1849. By the time locomotive production ended at Schenectady, in January of 1969, over 90,000 steam, electric, and diesel locomotives had been built by ALCO and its predecessor companies. The Canadian plant, Montreal Locomotive Works, continued to build locomotives until 1985.

Gettysburg Railroad RS 3 1555 was at Kane, Pa., in October 1982. The locomotive was used for a while when Sloan Cornell took over operations of the ex-B&O Mt. Jewett-to-Knox branch line, and portions of the Pennsy Erie-to-Emporium line. The 1600 hp., RS3 is powered by a 12-cylinder, 244D engine. It was a good seller for ALCO, with 1272 built between 1950 and 1956. Montreal Locomotive Works would also build 146 RS3's between 1951 and 1955. By comparison, between 1950 and 1959, GM built 2,615 1500 hp., GP7's and 3,601 1750 hp., GP9's in the United States. 112 GP7's and 645 GP9's were also built at GM's Canadian subsidiary, General Motors Diesel.

Knox and Kane Railroad RS36 70 is shown northbound at Chaffee, on January 12, 1998. The RS36 model was built between 1962 and 1963, with 40 built for seven railroads. Powered by a 12 cylinder, 1800 hp., 251C engine, the model superseded the RS11 with better electrical components and air filtration systems.

Delaware & Hudson C420 420 was at Moscow, Pa., on November 3, 1985, on Steamtown's ex-Lackawanna mainline. The C420 was the first of ALCO's Century Series locomotives, producing 2000 hp., with a 12-cylinder 251C engine. 131 were built between 1963 and 1968 for thirteen railroads. ALCO stopped U.S. production in 1969 for many reasons. As with the other steam locomotive builders, ALCO was slow to respond to GM's successful, early, passenger E-units and freight FT's. World War II restricted any new locomotive design production by the War Production Board. While GM continued to produce their FT's, ALCO was producing steam locomotives for the power-short railroads in the U.S. When the war was over, ALCO rushed its new 244 engines into production on its new road locomotives without enough service testing, resulting in low reliability and high maintenance. By the time ALCO released their improved 251 engine, in 1954, many railroads were reluctant to reorder from ALCO. With GE's success with their Universal Series in the early 1960s, they became the number-two builder. With the conditions of the U.S. railroads in the 1960s, there weren't enough orders to support three builders. Despite ALCO's departure in 1969, it's still possible to see these locomotives still operation on short lines and industrial railroads, 40-, 50-, and even 60-years after they rolled out of Schenectady.

Chapter 13
Remnants of the Western Maryland Railway

A trip to the Elkins, West Virginia, in September 2003, revealed remnants of the Western Maryland Railway. The Durbin & Greenbrier Valley Railroad at Durbin also operates two more excursion routes in the area. From Belington, the New Tygart Flyer excursion train runs 17 miles east on former B&O track, for which the Western Maryland had trackage rights to Elkins. From here, the train ran 23 miles up Cheat Mountain, on the former Western Maryland, to the High Falls on the Shavers Fork of the Cheat River. From the Falls, a motor car, which is a replica of a 1922 Edwards Railway Motor Car and was built in 2000, runs 38 miles south, through the abandoned town of Spruce and on to the 4066' Summit Cut, the highest mainline railroad crossing in the eastern U.S. The line continues to Webster Springs, but is currently out of service.

Occasionally the excursion train runs west from Belington 11 ½ miles to Tygart Junction. Motive power in 2003 included two former Western Maryland engines, BL2 #82 and FA2 #303, also an FP7 and an F7B from the Clinchfield Railroad. In the late 1940s, the railroads were looking for a higher horsepower locomotive to run alone on branch lines, which could run forward and reverse with good visibility, and have front and rear platforms to make switching easier.

GM would take their F-unit, taper the rear of the engine body hood and nose, which would allow the engineer to see crew members on the front and back and would do away with the need to turn the engine at the end of a branch line. 59 of the BL2's were built between 1948 and 1949. Western Maryland acquired two of the "no mistaking them for anything else" 1500 hp. engines in 1949. With the introduction of the GP7 in the late 1949, GM discontinued production on the BL2. Western Maryland would acquire from ALCO four FA2's in January 1951, road numbers 301 to 304. Powered by a 12-cylinder 244D, the engines were rated at 1600 hp.

After 20 years of service on the WM, the FA2's were sold to GE, then acquired by the Long Island Railroad and converted to push/pull service on their commuter lines. 52 years after leaving Schenectady, 303 is back in WM territory, minus its prime mover and traction motors. The engine still has its operating controls, allowing it to operate using the trailing engine's power.
Here one sees BL2 82's unique profile as it sets at Belington, on September 3, 2003. WVC are the operating initials of the line (West Virginia Central). Western Maryland's other BL2 81 is at the B&O Museum in Baltimore, Maryland.

82 runs around the excursion train to push it the final miles uphill to the High Falls, on September 4, 2003. A photo from the cab window on the BL2 would reveal the changes GM made in the engine body, by comparing the lines of trailing F7B 415. The narrowed body would give visibility down the track, and the slopping ridge allowed engineers to see crew members more easily.
On September 4, 2003, FA2 303 prepares to take the New Tygart Flyer to the High Falls from Belington. The engines run around the train on the way to the High Falls in the center photo. When the train returned to Belington, the engines would cut off the train and hook up to 33 hopper and gondola cars for Elkins.

A look back to the 1960s era on the Western Maryland is had as the three engines depart Belington. Like many railroads that disappeared before and after a merger, it must have been a hard loss for people with an interest, and communities who lost rail service, when the Western Maryland was swallowed up by Chessie System, and most of its route miles were abandoned.

At Belington, on September 11, 2004, the two former Clinchfield F-units and BL2 82 were stopped in the yard. 67 and 82 took the train that day up the 2.5% ruling grade to High Falls. WM never owned an FP7, instead relying on four high, short hood RS-3's for what little passenger service remained in the 1950s. The FP7 is four feet longer than the standard F7, to provide room for the steam generator and boiler that provided steam heat for the passenger cars. FP7 67 (ex-Clinchfield 200) was numbered next in sequence, with WM's first F7's ordered in 1950 (53-66), just as F7B 415 (ex-Clinchfield 869) was next in sequence to WM's F7B's (401-414).

The Western Maryland Scenic Railroad operates 17 miles of WM's Connellsville Subdivision between Cumberland and Frostburg, Md. An ex-Lake Superior & Ishpeming Railroad 2-8-0, built by Baldwin in 1916, and two GP30 (former Pennsy and Reading) engines power the trains. The heavy consolidation is numbered 734, representing the H-7A class of 2-8-0s (707-736) operated by the WM. They were built by ALCO in 1911. The 212-ton engine produces 60,480 lbs. of tractive effort, making it well suited for the 1.75% grade that climbs 1300 feet. A short, 2.8% grade of the old Cumberland and Pennsylvania Railway is used to reach the end of the line at Frostburg.
Here, GP30 502 brings a train downhill around Helmstetter's Curve, on September 18, 2004. A cab ride up the hill on 734 earlier in the day provided a combination of sound, sight, smell, and motion in complete contrast to the GP30s muffled 567 V-16, and the whining of dynamic brakes.

Growing up in the 1970s, my only acquaintance with the Western Maryland was seeing an occasional GP7 or GP9 on the B&O, Mt. Jewett-to-Knox, Pa. branchline. Over the years, cab rides on ex-WM engines and lines have raised my interest of the railroad. An unobstructed picture-window view is seen from West Virginia Central ex-WM BL2 82 as it heads west to Elkins, returning from High Falls, on September 12, 2003.

Engine 734 gives a good representation of the railroad as it rounds Helmstetter's Curve westbound, on September 19, 2004. What a remarkable spot this location must have been in the early 1950s. WM trains leaving Cumberland might have an M-2 Class 4-6-6-4 on the point, a I-2 Class 2-10-0 cut in the middle, and another I-2 shoving on the back. In the unlikely event you would grow tired of the WM Fireball, B&O's Sand Patch Grade was a few miles away, with EM-1 2-8-8-4's and S-1 2-10-2 "Big Sixes" engaged in the same battle of moving tonnage out of Cumberland.

Western Maryland Scenic Railroad began operations in the spring of 1991. Power to start was loaned FPA4, RS3, and RSD5. 734 arrived in July 1992, and the two ex-Conrail GP30s in 1995. Two miles of track had to be relayed to Frostburg, from the junction known as "Numer Nine," which leaves the now-abandoned line to Connellsville. These last two miles are on the former Cumberland and Pennsylvania Railway. The C&P was built before the Civil War, from Cumberland, through Frostburg, and on to Westernport to reach the coal fields in the Georges Creek Valley. WM would acquire the line in 1944.
At Frostburg an ex-WM, 100-foot turntable, from Elkins, W.Va. was installed, allowing the turning of engines for the return trip to Cumberland.

The short, squared off nose of West Virginia Central ex-WM FA2 303 heads east through a deep cut between Elkins and High Falls, on September 12, 2003. In steam days, six of WM's heavy Consolidations could be assembled to take a 65-car coal train east, out of Elkins to Cumberland, for the 3.05%-grade to Thomas. By mid-1954, five RS2's and fourteen RS3's would dieselize the Thomas Subdivision, doing away with the last of WM's H-Class 2-8-0s.

On May 27, 2005, the 734 has been turned and is about to run around the train. Once back at Cumberland, 734 would be cut from the train and run to Maryland Junction to turn on a wye. With GP30 501 switching cars in the yard on 734's return, the engineer decided to run to the station for water. The 1913 WM passenger station provides the backdrop as 734's tender is topped off. South of the station the railroad crosses the Potomac River, entering Ridgeley, W.V. where the former WM car shop and yard is used to maintain the equipment.

Opened to traffic in 1912, the 86-mile Connellsville Subdivision was an early casualty from the formation of Chessie System. Through traffic was switched over to B&O's Sand Patch line, in May 1975. In the 1960s, the line was still busy, with four scheduled eastbounds and four scheduled westbounds daily, plus coal, ore, and grain extras. Here, Western Maryland Scenic Railroad GP30 501 headed east, with a Cumberland-bound train at Brush Tunnel, on May 26, 2005. I can visualize a cab ride in 1950, on a new set of WM F7's in full dynamics, keeping the speed in check on eastbound train. A volcano of smoke and steam erupt as one of WM's big Challengers emerges from the 914' Brush Tunnel, bringing a freight train up the 1.75% grade on the now-removed, westbound main. Better close all the cab windows, in case of passing the lead helper in the double-track bore. About a mile after exiting the tunnel, Helmstetter's Curve gives you a chance to look out the left side of the black fireball covered wagon, to check the progress of your train. But before that, the second helper will pass on the westbound, shoving against a bright red, WM caboose. Added at Cumberland, the helpers stayed with the train for the 22-mile climb to the summit at Deal, gaining almost 1,700' in elevation. Will there ever be another railroad quite like the "Wild Mary"?

Ex-L.S. & I, R.R. 2-8-0 34 sets at Ridgeley Yard on May 29, 2005. With its large boiler, 56" drive wheels, and six axle tender from a New York Central 4-8-2 Mohawk, 734 looks at home on the ex-WM rails. Maryland Junction at the south end of Ridgeley Yard was the junction where the railroad branched to the west on the Thomas Sub to Elkins, and east on the West Subdivision to Hagerstown.

GP30 501, ex-PRR 2249 was at Frostburg, on May 26, 2005. The engine was one of 52 GP30s built for the Pennsylvania Railroad in 1963, and was the third from the last locomotive to be delivered to the railroad with trainphone antennas. Above the dynamic brake blister, barely visible, are the brackets that supported the antennas, confirming its Pennsy heritage. Despite that Western Maryland didn't have any GP30s objections from some WM fans, the fact must be appreciated that one can still ride the cab of a black, speed-lettered, four-axle EMD along a portion of the Connellsville Sub, which was WM's onetime gateway to the west.

GP30 502, ex-Reading 5507, is westbound as it rounds Helmstetter's Curve, on May 26, 2005. The engine was one of 20 GP30s built for the Reading Railroad in 1962.

About one mile uphill, 502 is about to enter the east entrance of Brush Tunnel. While the line was double-tracked from Georges Creek Junction 18 miles to Colmar, the rest of the line to Connellsville was mostly single track. The WM had great hopes for the line and during construction, bridges and tunnels were built to accommodate a second track. The line was better engineered than Sand Patch, built 40 years previous, but was unable to draw enough traffic away from the B&O to justify extending the double track west. Surprisingly, this WM mainline would last little less than 63 years as a through route.

On May 28, 2005, instead of trying to chase the Western Maryland Scenic train from Cumberland to Frostburg, I decided to go to Brush Tunnel. Departing Cumberland at 11:30 A.M., the train reaches the tunnel shortly before noon. After checking for copperheads, I'm on top of the east portal of the tunnel as 734 brings the train uphill westbound. The Pennsy train phone antenna brackets are clearly visible along the top of 501 as it gives the train a push.

A three hour wait for the return trip would give me time to look the tunnel over. I discovered a small length of rail in the 20 lb. per yard or less that was no doubt from a narrow gauge line used to haul debris from the tunnel during construction. 501 would be in charge of the eastbound run. An "atta boy" has to be given for the operators of this line and the Elkins W.Va. area line that help keep the Western Maryland Railway heritage alive.

Back at Belington, West Virginia, on September 22, 2005, West Virginia Central FA2 303 was in a siding while BL2 82 and FP7 67 prepare to take the New Tygart Flyer to High Falls.

On the return trip from High Falls, 67's cab provides a good view along the former B&O right of way, between Elkins and Belington, on September 22, 2005.

The New Tygart Flyer runs on track that was used for coal trains through the 1980s and consists of mostly welded rail. On September 23, 2005, BL2 82 heads the train to High Falls twelve miles east of Belington.

About thirteen miles after leaving High Falls, 67 and 82 head downhill as they pass through Bowden, on September 23, 2005. Like the Western Maryland, by the early 1950s Clinchfield Railroad passenger service was just about over. A single order to GM in February 1952, for FP7 200, was all that would be needed until passenger service was discontinued in April 1954. The engine would then work in freight service and occasional excursion service. Working for Clinchfield, Family Lines System, Seaboard System, CSX, and now West Virginia Central, the locomotive has been in operation for 53 years. The open area between the fuel tank and lead truck shows that 67 has lost its water tank and steam boiler, and is now listed as an F7 on West Virginia Central's roster. The boxcar behind the engines has a generator to provide power for the cars.

67 and 82 are westbound with the return trip, twelve miles east of Belington, on September 23, 2005.

Western Maryland Shay 6 was at Cass, West Virginia, on September 24, 2005. With the cylinders and drive shafts located on the right side of Shays, very few people photograph the left side of the locomotives, which seem to have a somewhat unfinished look to them.

A close-up view of WM 6 at Cass, on September 24, 2005, shows how the off-set boiler leaves the fireman with limited views ahead. 6's 48" wheels and heavy frame are quite apparent, as the big 162-ton locomotive prepares to shove another train up the mountain.

Living within 50 miles from where they were built at Corry, Pa., I've always had an interest in Climax Locomotives. A return trip to Durbin, W.Va., on September 24, 2005, revealed Durbin & Greenbrier Valley's (ex-Moore-Keppel & Company) #3 steaming in the yard. 3's front and rear drive shafts to each truck can be seen under the locomotive. At 55 tons, the locomotive is over 100 tons less than the "Big Six" at Cass.

Although the ex-C&O Greenbrier Division rails between Cass and Durbin are in place, washouts prevent operation of the entire distance. Five miles south of Durbin, which is as far as 3 can operate, it is shown waiting for the return trip to Durbin, on September 24, 2005. The narrow-gauge, Tionesta Valley Railway's mainline passed within 1000 feet from where I live It operated Climaxes of the vintage of 3 built in 1910. From stories my granddad told of working for the TVRY, and from seeing the 3 under steam, I can visualize one of their 40-ton Climaxes pausing long enough to take on water before continuing on to Sheffield with another train of logs.

Chapter 14
A Final Look

Pennsylvania Railroad

My first encounter with the Pennsylvania Railroad was in 1965, when I was four. It was the first part of March when my dad took my mom, two sisters, and me to Warren, Pa. to ride one of the last passenger trains east to Kane on Pennsy's Erie-to-Emporium line. The daily Northern Express 581 westbound and 580 eastbound ended service on March 27, 1965.

The heart of the 10,000 mile Pennsylvania Railroad was the 245 miles of four-track mainline between Pittsburgh and Harrisburg, with Altoona located at the center. This photo shows GP40-2 3299 leaving Altoona and onto the Middle Division with an eastbound train on July 24, 1981. Conrail had 272 GP40s and 128 GP40-2's. The coat of Conrail Blue can't hide the identity of the ex-Pennsy N5c caboose on the back of an empty coal train.

Back on the Horseshoe Curve, B23-7's 2021, 2020, two GM's, and another GE on eastbound train, May 24, 1980. Conrail received 141 of the 2250 hp engines from GE between 1977 and 1979.

Norfolk Southern, ex-Conrail, 3332 was at Altoona, Pa., on October 6, 2001. Conrail started with 118 SD40s, and by 1979 another 167 SD40-2 would be added. With the Conrail split on June 1, 1999, Norfolk Southern took control of mostly former Pennsy lines, and CSX took mostly former New York Central lines. Norfolk Southern would apply PRR, and CSX would apply NYC initials on their equipment to show ownership.
Over 150 years have passed since the Pennsylvania Railroad first arrived in the Altoona area, and at least until the ex-Conrail engines and cars are repainted, the PRR will still be a part of the scene. This side view of 3332 provides a good look at its long, front porch. GM would use the 68' 10", SD45-2 frame on the SD40-2's. With a shorter engine hood resulting from four fewer cylinders, the engines had distinctive, long, front and back platforms.

Although the Pennsylvania Railroad had a bigger dominance in the state, the B&O made a bigger impact on me. Living within three miles of the Mt. Jewett-to-Knox branchline, the B&O was more accessible.

In the 1970s the crew based out of Marienville would run north to Mt. Jewett on Tuesday, Thursday, and Saturday, and south to Knox on Monday, Wednesday, and Friday. By the late 1970s, trains would average two GP9's and twenty to thirty cars, mostly carrying coal. By the early 1980s, the coal traffic dried up, along with the closing of the glass plant at Marienville. With little traffic, the line was scheduled for abandonment. Fortunately, the line would survive.

GP9's 6479 and 6478 with a short southbound train were near Sheffield Junction, in June 1978. 6478 is still in as-delivered colors, with B&O spelled out on the long hood and yellow strip.

My dog George's instinct seems to be telling him there is a feline in the area. If he would look up, he would be face-to-face with the sound-asleep Chessie the Cat, on the front of GP7 5629 resting with a southbound work train, two miles north of Sheffield Junction, in August of 1981. The engine was one of seven passenger GP7's that the B&O ordered in 1953. Nineteen passenger GP9's would follow in 1956. The normal freight GP7's and GP9's had two large air tanks mounted cross-ways, between the fuel tank and truck, under the long hood. In the passenger engines, this space occupied the water tank for the steam generator. With space inside and underneath used up, GM would place four long narrow air tanks on top of the locomotive. Not surprisingly, these engines would aquire the nickname "Torpedo Geeps."

GP9 6014 is shown northbound, one mile north of Sheffield Junction, in August 1978. 6014 was originally a Chesapeake & Ohio engine, but was transferred to the B&O in 1978. C&O had their Geeps set up to operate short hood forward, and the bell hung from the top of the hood. B&O preferred operating their Geeps long hood forward, theorizing it would give crews better protection in a collision. One thing about the Chessie colors, they would stand out at a grade crossing.

As with other railroads that operated in western Pennsylvania, the B&O had its share of operating problems during the winter months. In a January 1978 snowstorm, GP9's 6502 and 6560 are going northbound, with a coal train at Iron City crossing, one mile south of Watson Farm.

The train was making slow progress, and is shown here three miles later nearing Sheffield Junction.

The train crew would run out of hours and would return south on the following day. At the Iron City crossing the next morning, the two GP9's are Marienville-bound on a much calmer day.

My dog Jeff appears to have had enough rail-fanning for one day, as a southbound train sets out-of-hours at Russell City, in January of 1979. 5601 was one of 25 GP7's the B&O received in 1953 for freight service. Known for its numerous mountain grades, one wonders why the railroad didn't order these locomotives with dynamic brakes.

Occasionally, the B&O would operate large trains on the branchline. On March 11, 1978, GP9 6430 led three more GP9's, forty loads of coal, and eight mixed cars north, at the Watson Farm rock cut.

Hagerstown chop nose GP7 5632 was on a northbound train south of Sheffield Junction, in late March 1978. Before Chessie renumbering, the engine was number 20, the first of four GP7's on the Western Maryland, delivered in 1950. The GP7's, two BL2's, and five RS2's were the odd men out on the mountainous WM, being the only road engines lacking dynamic brakes.

One mile south of Sheffield Junction, in June 1981, B&O GP7 5978 is on a short, northbound train. The bell and C decal on its short hood indicate another ex-Chesapeake and Ohio engine. As with many railroads in the 1950s that wanted to drop the fires on their remaining steam locomotives, C&O turned to GM for 199 GP7's and 363 GP9's.

The Knox and Kane acquired Western Maryland GP9 6414 from Chessie System, and here it is shown at Byramtown, with five boxcars southbound, in March 1982. Despite the Western Maryland Railway's small size, it developed a large following. With many of its routes paralleled by the B&O, the WM always seemed to be the underdog.

The engine with new paint and numbered 14 is on the Kinzua Bridge-bound excursion train, one mile north of Nansen, on October 25, 1987. As with C&O, WM's GP7's and GP9's were set up to operate short hood forward.

On June 14, 1997, the engine was back on the Knox and Kane line with its original WM number, but still lettered for the Gettysburg Railroad. The train was heading southbound, two miles north of Russell City.

The top of a boxcar in the Nansen siding provides a good vantage point as Allegheny Railroad CF7 104 (originally built in 1951 as Santa Fe F7 264 L) powers the northbound excursion train, on August 9, 1992. Earlier in the month, 58 was involved in a collision with a truck at the Route 219 crossing at Lantz Corners, and 104 would substitute while 58 underwent repairs. In the early 1970s, the Santa Fe was looking for an alternative to buying new, low horsepower, road switchers. They would end up rebuilding 233 F3's and F7's into 1500 hp., CF7's at their Cleburne, Texas, shops between 1970 and 1978. With a lot of the strength built into the car body of the F-units, the Santa Fe would have to manufacture new frames for the engines. 104 was an earlier conversion, with the cab roof being part of the F-unit car body. CF7 2590 is shown with Bessemer & Lake Erie SD9 843 earlier in the book (see page 138), and is a later version with a squared-off, high, flat cab roof. 2590 was built in 1953 as Santa Fe F7 269L. Both CF7's were transferred to the Louisiana & Delta Railroad, owned by Genesee & Wyoming Industries.

Can anyone think of a better way to spend a late spring afternoon than in the cab of a 44-year old GP9, rocking down the old B&O branch line passing through Russell City, on June 8, 2001? Hard to believe, but it's been almost 25 years since, on June 22, 1976, at this spot, a train crew stopped and gave me a cab ride to Kane in B&O GP9 6439.

ALCO S6 44 hauled a Marienville-bound train one mile north of Sheffield Junction, on July 14, 1996. 44 would come to the Knox & Kane in 1988, after years of working the steel mills and industries of the Buffalo, N.Y. area, for Bethlehem Steel's South Buffalo Railway.

One mile south of Sheffield Junction, on October 8, 2004, RS36 70 takes two empty, center beam flatcars north, to the Buffalo & Pittsburgh interchange at Mt. Jewett. B&O did have several classes of ALCO S type switchers, as well as FA and FB road engines. With its clean lines and long, low nose, it would be tough to beat the looks of this 1962 product of Schenectady.

The Nickel Plate Road would use their PA1's as trade-ins to ALCO for eleven RS36's. Components from the eleven passenger engines, which were built in 1947 and 1948, were reused in the new RS36's. In 1881 the New York, Chicago & St. Louis Railroad was having financial trouble and was placed for sale. Railroad Baron Jay Gould would place a low bid, and was urged by interested parties to increase his bid. He said it wouldn't be raised even if the rails were nickel plated. Later in the railroad's life, the Nickel Plate Road was officially used. The 2,200 mile railroad would be one of the earlier merger casualties when it was taken over by the Norfolk & Western Railway, in October 1964. This photo shows 70 going northbound, with eight loads, one mile north of Nansen, on August 25, 1997.

The "High Speed Service" line was nearly gone, and the "Bluebirds," for over four decades, as 70 heads northbound at the Watson Farm rockcut, with four cars, on February 11, 2003. Thirty years have passed since I first started photographing this line. What changes the next thirty years will bring to this line, or the entire North American rail system, is anybody's guess.

Two and one-half miles north of Sheffield Junction, on October 21, 2001, 58 and 39 double-head a heavy southbound excursion train, at the top of Chaffee Hill.

Rails would span the Kinzua Valley and Creek near Mt. Jewett for 121 years, until the tornado of July 21, 2003. The remains, of what at one time was the highest railroad bridge in the world, stood firm on a snowless December 2 in 2004.

39 is shown northbound with six boxcars of particle board and one empty center beam flatcar, on February 15, 2005, one mile south of Russell City. Knox & Kane would continue excursions to the Kinzua bridge through October 2004. With the collapse of the bridge, ridership on the train fell to where it was no longer feasible to operate. Freight service would continue until January 2006, when the railroad voluntarily ceased operation due to poor track conditions. Engines 38, 58, and 39 would be moved to Kane and stored in the engine house. On March 16, 2008, an arson fire damaged the locomotives and an 1890s wooden passenger car, ending what little hope had been left to resume excursion trains to the Kinzua Bridge. On October 10th and 11th, 2008, all rolling stock and miscellaneous railroad materials were auctioned off. Kovalchick Salvage Company acquired the tracks and property, bringing an end to the Knox and Kane Railroad.

Besides the Knox & Kane's 58, two other Mikados were built in China, in 1989, for North American railroads. SY Class 1647 for the Connecticut Valley Railroad and JS Class 8419, which is larger than the SY Class, for the Boone & Scenic Valley Railroad at Boone, Iowa. 58 is shown northbound passing the Russell City water tank, on a snowy October 27, 2001.

A final look at the Knox and Kane finds 58 emerging from the fog on the morning of July 1, 1995, one mile north of Russell City, with a Kinzua Bridge-bound train.

As with ALCO's PA's, many considered the FA's to be better looking, when compared to GM's and the other builders' engines of the time. Between 1946 and 1959, ALCO built 1354 of the four-axle FA's, from the FA1's to the FPA4. By comparison, GM would build around 7,600 four-axle F-units between 1939 and 1959.
Western Maryland FA2 303 was at Belington, West Virginia, on September 4, 2003. Even with all of the scrapes and dents of 52 years of road service, it would still be tough to improve on the solid, squared-off profile of the FA2.

Buffalo & Pittsburgh GP38 2001, three SD45's, and Allegheny and Eastern GP40 302 bring a long, southbound train uphill, two miles north of Mt. Jewett, Pa., on May 17, 1996.

25,000 AC horsepower in the form of five Norfolk Southern SD80MAC's, one-sixth the total production, head west from Cresson, Pa. to work the coal branchlines in the Johnstown area, on May 11, 2003. One has received a coat of NS black, while the other four remain in Conrail Blue. At 210 tons, 80'2" in length, and 5000 hp., these are NS's largest locomotives. These engines have a 185,000 lb. starting, and 147,000, lb. continuous tractive effort. The grand total of the five are a length of 400' 10", 1050 tons, 925,000 lb. starting, and 735,000 lb. continuous tractive effort. A person has to wonder if they will be able to assemble enough loaded hoppers to put these engines to the test.

Index